, è tre Violoncelli , col Basso per il Cembalo .

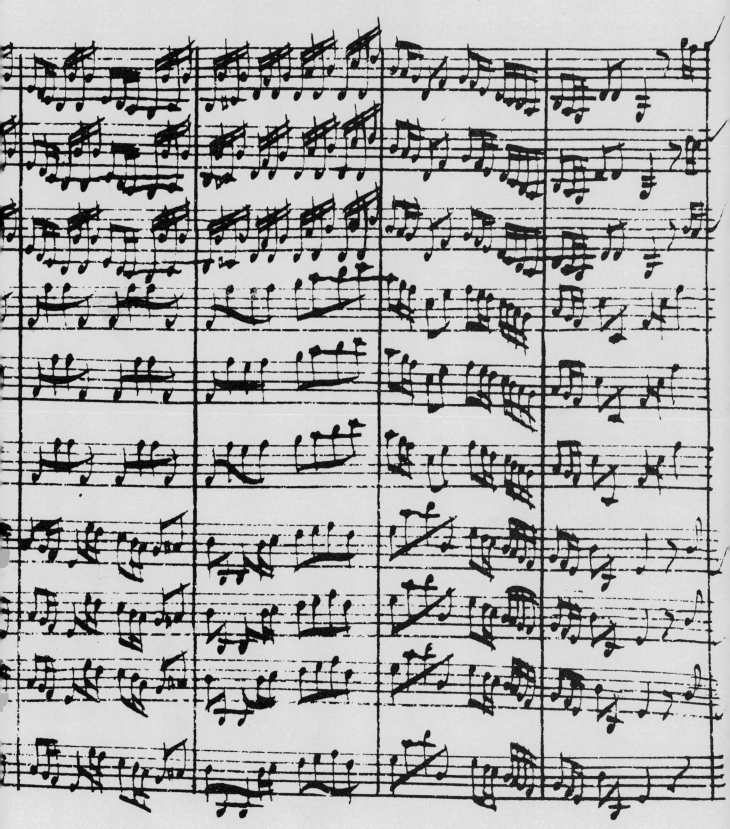

WERNER FELIX

JOHANN
SEBASTIAN
BACH

WERNER FELIX

JOHANN SEBASTIAN BACH

W.W. Norton & Company
New York   London

For Beate

© VEB Deutscher Verlag für Musik, Leipzig, 1984
© English text: Orbis Publishing Limited, 1985
First American edition, 1985
All rights reserved

ISBN 0-393-02232-3

W.W. Norton & Company, Inc., 500 Fifth Avenue,
New York, New York 10110
W.W. Norton & Company, Ltd, 37 Great Russell Street,
London WC1B 3NU

Printed in the German Democratic Republic

1 2 3 4 5 6 7 8 9 0

Contents

Foreword

"This Leipzig cantor," wrote Zelter to Goethe, "is an apparition of God!" Indeed, Bach was propelled by genius above the clouds where mortals find the air too rarefied for existence. His works will be well discussed and the stations of his life retailed in this book, but no one can explain how this Saxon-Thuringian artisan-artist appeared and took his place securely in history as the *musicus maximus*, a title we must accept at its full value.

Issue of a remarkable line of musicians, mostly provincial organists, municipal pipers and fiddlers (although also including a few fine composers), Bach never spurned his origins, and remained faithful to the traditions of this hereditary clan, but with a barely perceptible flicker and only half-disclosed gestures, distanced himself subtly from anything routine or banal. Although he did have social ambitions and wanted to be a court composer and Kapellmeister, he respected the family vocation of service as church musicians, and in that customary everyday work he endeavoured to carry the cantor's art to its apogee. Even as a very young man he was convinced that a professional should know his métier from alpha to omega, witness his determination to hear and study the famous living masters. He undertook long trips, sometimes because of his modest circumstances, on foot, to hear such famous organists as Reinken and Buxtehude. This quest for knowledge remained with him to the end, and this mastery of the métier became so comprehensive that he could accommodate every method and procedure without disturbing the natural flow of his music. To him such mastery of the art of composing was a summons and a mandate.

There emerges from his oeuvre a picture of mind and heart in perfect equilibrium, where these two ancient partners and adversaries, always trying to separate themselves from each other yet always depending on mutual support, are at peace. Bach liked restrictions in construction, for they had to be overcome, and he obviously loved to pit his mind against challenges, but when we listen to the highly charged thunder of the strettos in his great fugues, our pulse quickens and we almost forget their flawless construction. We also discover that despite the élan and the overwhelming expressivity, Bach never permitted his inspiration to bypass his self-criticism in his endeavour to seize the truth and not its mere illusion. He knew his capabilities, we may hope even his role in history, and he always found the most suitable vessels to serve his ideas. Nothing was tentative, nothing of what he wanted to say was lost, and he could illuminate his truth from every angle, in every mode of musical speech without getting embroiled in a galimatias. That this marvellous plasticity of form and range of expression was deliberately confined to genres that were already half extinct, is what baffles us.

All around Bach the musical world was changing and even his own highly gifted sons failed to understand his aims and ideas. That we have good copies of many of the manuscripts that Carl Philipp Emanuel and Friedemann Bach recklessly lost or sold we owe to his many disciples. He was indeed a thorough and sympathetic teacher whose students, many living in the warm atmosphere of his household, lovingly and loyally kept his memory fresh during the days when he was temporarily forgotten.

Bach was fully aware that the age of polyphony was passing and he was familiar with the new trends and fashions. Still, he tried with unparalleled energy and consistency to keep the old polyphony alive. Why? Unfortunately, since he never recorded his personal aims, we can only explore and present them at some scholarly risk.

Bach's instrumental music, the great Passion oratorios, and the cantatas (though not nearly enough of the latter) have long since become known, loved, and appreciated, but the works of his last period are difficult fare for many, even some of the composer's most ardent admirers. The reasons for the change in style and mood are twofold, the first due to circumstances. With the installation of a new, Neo-humanist rector at the Thomas-schule not only a new regime but an entirely new concept of education was initiated, one in which music no longer played the role to which the conservative Bach was accustomed. Rector Ernesti wanted to emphasize Classical learning and discipline, and Bach's authority was severely curtailed. The situation became so hostile that Bach virtually retired to his study, and though he discharged his duties his heart was no longer in them. Still, his study hummed with concentrated work not intended for profane eyes. The second reason for the change in direction lay in Bach's compelling desire to gather his works into orderly collections, to sum up and codify all he had learned of the forms and idioms handed down to him. Presently he returned to where he had started, keyboard music – that is, a type of music he and the initiated could handle by themselves.

One after the other of the artistic *summae* were created: the second book of *The Well Tempered Clavier*; *The Art of Fugue*; the variations *Vom Himmel Hoch*; and the *Ars canonica*, later called (though not by Bach) *A Musical Offering*; he finished the *Clavier-Übung* and completed the tremendous anthology we know today as the B Minor Mass (also not so named by Bach). All these were really *Kunstbücher*, repositories into which Bach entered all the wisdom and experience gained during his artistic career. He felt that in his earlier works he had achieved everything that he wanted to do in the spirit of his forebears, but now he clearly wanted nothing less than to reach the last boundaries of the musical cosmos. In this unheard-of endeavour canon and fugue naturally represented the counterpoise between the world and the beyond, between time and eternity. Many feel that in these mighty works Bach composed for a small élite to whom the ancient secrets were known; Dahlhaus rightly called such works as *The Art of Fugue* creations for other composers to learn from. True, but they are accessible to us if we study every canon and fugue lovingly; they are independent entities and what defeats the unwary is the assumption that these collections are multi-movement compositions. It is not even certain that they were meant for public performance, and certainly not to be heard in one sitting. It takes a lifetime to become familiar with these, but it is a life well spent.

There is another thing we must understand. In these works of his last period, Bach is not thinking about polyphony, but about thinking itself: thinking in the incorporeal language of music, spare and unadorned. We should bear in mind what Rodin said: "In the arts to admit only what we understand leads to impotence."

Bach has been called the "Gothic Bach", the "mathematical Bach", and he has been seen as the translator of Euclid into music, but many saw him, above all, as the German religious mystic. Indeed, following Schweitzer the hermeneutists based their works on this assumption and are still looking for unexplained profound meanings behind every note. The symbolism is, of course, present in this music, even involved numerology, because ever since the Middle Ages religious mysticism lived in German arts and letters; but we as musicians must always look at the music *qua* music. That music flows irresistibly, totally unhindered by anything extramusical, for it is really entirely obedient to music's own laws. We cannot fathom Bach's inner beliefs and ideals, for the mysticism was his very private possession, solely for himself. In any case, where psychology in the arts begins there are no longer deeds, only motives for deeds; man speaks in perfect sentences only when fully conscious, and in Bach's case this consciousness was primarily musical.

Great creations of the past do not perish; they may be eclipsed for a time but come back and live more intensely and convincingly when they conjure up forgotten experiences. "The poet," says Goethe, "releases his creations into the world, it is up to us, the beholders, to find out what he intended to communicate." This is our still unfinished task. We honour ourselves and vastly enhance our understanding and therefore our enjoyment of the music of this giant among composers if we cultivate his memory and try to solve the many questions and problems he left for posterity to unravel. But as we do so we should never forget that we are dealing with a musician, an incarnation of the creative artist, and it is in the music itself we must find the answers.

Paul Henry Lang

Johann Sebastian Bach – Chronology

1685	21 March	Johann Sebastian Bach born in Eisenach
	22 March	Baptized in St George's Church
1693–1695		Attends the Latin School
1694	3 May	Burial of his mother, Elisabeth Bach, *née* Lämmerhirt
1695	20 February	Death of his father, Johann Ambrosius Bach
1696–1700		Attends the Lyceum, Ohrdruf
1700–1702		Attends St Michael's School, Lüneburg
1702		Unsuccessful candidacy for post as organist at St Jacob's, Sangerhausen
1703	March–September	Musician at the court of Johann Ernst of Saxe-Weimar
	9 August	Appointment as organist at the New Church, Arnstadt
1705–1706		Three- to four-month trip to Lübeck
1707	15 June	Appointment as organist at Divi Blasii, Mühlhausen
	17 October	Marriage to Maria Barbara Bach
1708	June	Appointment as organist and *Kammermusiker* at the court of the Dukes Wilhelm Ernst and Ernst August of Saxe-Weimar
	29 December	Baptism of daughter, Catharina Dorothea
1710	22 November	Birth of son, Wilhelm Friedemann
1713	February	Trip to ducal court at Weissenfels
	December	Audition as organist in Halle
1714	February	Rejects offer from Halle
	2 March	Named *Konzertmeister* at Weimar
	8 March	Birth of son, Carl Philipp Emanuel
1715	11 May	Birth of son, Johann Gottfried Bernhard
1716	28 April–2 May	Tests the organ at Our Lady's Church, Halle
1717	5 August	Named *Kapellmeister* at the court of Prince Leopold of Anhalt-Cöthen
	Autumn	Trip from Weimar to Dresden for projected competition playing against Louis Marchand
	6 November	Arrest in Weimar as a result of his emphatic demands for discharge from service at Weimar
	2 December	Discharge from prison and service at Weimar
	December	Moves to Cöthen
1718	May/June	Trip to Carlsbad
1720	End of May(?)– beginning of July	Trip to Carlsbad
	7 July	Burial of wife, Maria Barbara Bach, Cöthen (prior to Bach's return from Carlsbad)
	November	Trip to Hamburg, contests the post of organist at the Jakobikirche
1721	3 December	Marriage to Anna Magdalene Wilcke, Cöthen

1722	21 December	Candidacy for the post of cantor at St Thomas's, Leipzig
1723	7 February	Audition for post of cantor at St Thomas's Church in Leipzig
	13 April	Requests discharge from Prince Leopold
	22/23 April	Accepts post of cantor at St Thomas's
	5 May	Signs acknowledgement of employment
	22 May	Moves to Leipzig
	November	Testing and dedication of organ, Störmthal
1724	25 June	Testing and dedication of organ, Gera
1725	19/20 September	Recitals on the Silbermann organ at the Sophienkirche, Dresden
1727	19 November	Death of Prince Leopold of Anhalt-Cöthen
1729	End of March	Takes over directorship of the Collegium Musicum
1730	23 August	Petition to the Leipzig council of "Short, but most necessary outline for a well-appointed church music . . ."
1731	September	Concerts at the Sophienkirche and the court at Dresden; meets Johann Adolf Hasse
1732	April	Move into the converted and extended St Thomas's school
	September	Trip to Kassel, testing and dedication of organ at the Martinskirche
1733	July	Trip to Dresden; request (on 27 July) to be granted a court title by Elector Friedrich August II of Saxony, in a letter accompanying Mass, BWV 232
1735	5 September	Birth of son, Johann Christian
1736	July	Beginning of feud with Prefect
	1 December	Organ recital at Our Lady's Church, Dresden
1737	May	Johann Adolf Scheibe makes his first attack on Bach's compositional style
1738	January	Johann Abraham Birnbaum's first defence of Bach against Scheibe's criticism
1739	17 March	Performance of a Passion forbidden by Leipzig council
	November	Trip to Weissenfels
1741	August	Trip to Berlin
	November	Trip to Dresden
1742	31 October	Johann Elias Bach leaves the position held since 1737 as tutor and private secretary in Bach's household in Leipzig
1743	December	Tests organ at St John's Church, Leipzig
1745	30 November	Leipzig occupied by Prussian troops in the Second Silesian War
1746		Portrait of Johann Sebastian Bach painted in oils by Elias Gottlob Haussmann
	26/27 September	Tests and certifies organ at St Wenceslas' Church, Naumburg
1747	7/8 May	Visits the court of King Frederick II of Prussia, Potsdam
	June	Joins Society of Musical Sciences
1749	4 October	Birth of grandson, Johann Sebastian Altnickol (d. 21.12.1749)
1750	End of March	First eye operation
	Beginning of April	Second eye operation
	22 July	Last Communion
	28 July	Death of Johann Sebastian Bach
	30/31 July	Buried in St John's cemetery

1. Map of Thuringia, Saxony and Anhalt-Cöthen, 1734.

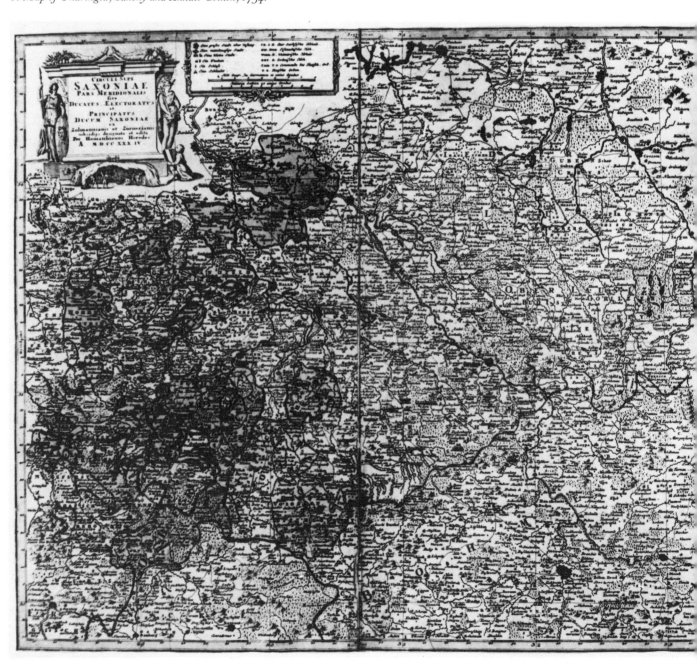

The Bach Family

In the history of Western music one family stands out as having produced, generation after generation, a succession of remarkably productive musicians: the Bach family, of whom the greatest was Johann Sebastian. Most of the Bachs seem to have lived in Thuringia, although records dating back hundreds of years show that families bearing this name were also to be found in Saxony, Franconia, Southern Germany, Bohemia, Moravia, Hungary, and Transylvania. In 1735, in Leipzig, Johann Sebastian himself drew attention to this phenomenon by compiling a comprehensive survey of all the musically active members of his family. The Bach family tree includes numerous cantors, organists, town musicians, schoolmasters, organ builders, musicians to city councils, court musicians, and others of similar occupation, and in many instances a single branch of the family was active in one place — Erfurt, for example — for several generations. An entry in the Lexicon of Music compiled by Johann Gottfried Walther, a cousin of Johann Sebastian, refers to the connection between the musical profession and the family name:

> . . .The Bach family is reputed to have originated in Hungary, and, as far as can be ascertained, all who have possessed this name have had a great affection for music; which may come from the fact that the very letters that form the name do them-selves form a melody — B A C H
> (Note: in German notation B represents the English B flat and H the English B.)

Some of the early major biographical studies suggest that musicians in Thuringia were referred to as "Bachs" simply because so many of them did in fact possess that name. However, recent research has revealed that in the vernacular "Bach" (also "Pach" and "Pachen") has many meanings.

In his family history Johann Sebastian Bach mentions at least forty-two members who had been professional musicians during the preceding two centuries, but the list cannot have been exhaustive. Many of the places he mentions, such as Gotha, Wechmar, Suhl, Erfurt, Weimar, Arnstadt, Eisenach, Gehren, Ohrdruf, Mühlhausen, Blankenhain, Jena, and Sondershausen, seem to point to Thuringia as a region especially favoured by the Bachs. In places outside this area, such as Schweinfurt, Königsberg, Stockholm, and Frankfurt-on-Oder, Bachs were less numerous. The places Bach mentions are frequently those in which he himself spent some time during his career, and the fact that he followed in the steps of his ancestors in this way confirms the fact that the Bachs had always, throughout the centuries, been a strongly-knit clan. We may also deduce that, had he chosen to do so, Bach could have revealed much more than he did about his ancestors'

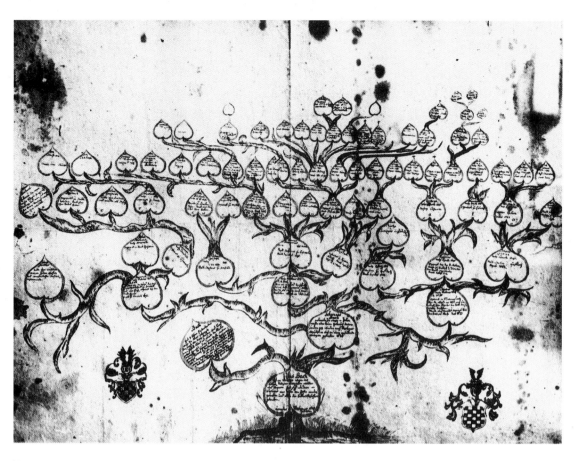

lives and attitudes in his concise and factual survey of 1735.

Johann Sebastian Bach belonged to the fifth generation of his family, counting the Vitus, or Veit Bach, with whom he began his narrative. Veit Bach, who died some time before 1577, had been a baker and miller in Wechmar near Gotha. Bach mentions his sojourn in Hungary and return to Thuringia, and writes affectionately about his ancestor's love of music. Veit's son Johannes (Hans) received his musical education from the town piper of Gotha and later settled in his birthplace, Wechmar, travelling on various occasions to Arnstadt, Schmalkalden, Eisenach and Suhl to help their local musicians. He died in 1626. His eldest son, Christoph (1613–61), having received a musical education, was employed as a court musician in Weimar, then moved to Erfurt (in 1642) and to Arnstadt (in 1654) as a member of their "Company of Musicians".

Christoph had three sons, two of whom were twins born in 1645: Johann Ambrosius and Johann Christoph, who died respectively in 1695 and 1693. Johann Ambrosius became a town musician of Erfurt in 1647 but later moved to Eisenach (1671) where he married Elisabeth Lämmerhirt. Six sons and three daughters were born to them. Their youngest son was Johann Sebastian, born on 21 March 1685.

This description of the direct line from Veit down to Johann Sebastian by no means presents a complete picture of the manifold branches of the Bach family. As generation succeeded prolific generation, the family spread further and further afield and carried the name Bach all over the region. Not all those who bore the name were necessarily connected with the family of musicians, but a close inspection of church registers reveals that the direct descendants of one Caspar Bach numbered over one thousand born between the middle of the seventeenth and the middle of the nineteenth centuries.

Although we can gain some sort of overall view of the Bachs, their interrelationships are too complex for us to form a completely clear picture. Bach himself, in his family history, only attempted to deal with a part of the family. Nevertheless, the impression we gain, of a great pyramid of musical Bachs, at whose lofty peak stands one Johann Sebastian, is clear enough.

Numerous, too, were the connections established between the Bach family and other musical families throughout their history. These came about through common social and professional interests, the education of the children, the assistance given by one musician to another, the performance of each other's works and through marriage.

The Bach family originated essentially from the provincial artisan class. They were simple craftsmen who earned their bread by providing music for town, church and court. Their competence extended also to the production of musical instruments, and long before Johann Sebastian's time his ancestors were building organs. This particular combination of skills flourished throughout the sixteenth and seventeenth centuries but later declined somewhat. Part and parcel of this strong family tradition of craftsmanship were the restrictions that it placed on an individual, who went, as a matter of course, wherever he might develop his skills in reasonable circumstances, or where a suitable vacancy had occurred — of which the family grapevine or friends would have informed him as soon as possible. In many cases this policy resulted in certain posts becoming the virtual property of the Bachs, where the reputation of one generation ensured the almost automatic succession of the next, who, in turn, further enhanced the family reputation.

3. Wechmar, near Gotha, where several members of the Bach family had lived in earlier generations.

A custom strongly reminiscent of the traditions of craft guilds was that of family reunions, held at more or less regular intervals in any one of the towns where a substantial number of Bachs were living. The venue would probably be determined not only by the concentration of numbers but by the presence of an important member of the family who was unable to travel, for example, and they served a variety of purposes: the settlement of bequests, the sorting out of disputes, the discussion of professional and personal matters, decisions about the training and career of younger members and the general strengthening of family ties. In his book *The Life, the Art, and the Works of Johann Sebastian Bach* (1802), Johann Nikolaus Forkel gives a graphic description of these gatherings:

> As it was impossible for them all to live in the same place, they liked to gather at least once a year probably in Erfurt, Eisenach or Arnstadt. Their favourite occupation during these gatherings was to engage in some form of musical activity. Naturally enough, as they were all choirmasters, organists or town musicians, connected in some way with the church, and also because custom demanded a religious framework, they would start with the singing of a chorale. This solemnity, however, would soon give way to more light-hearted music-making, which was often in strong contrast to what had gone before. They liked to sing folksongs of a light or sometimes ribald nature, singing two or more simultaneously and extemporizing upon them so that a sort of choral harmony resulted. These "quodlibets", as they called them, not only made the performers themselves laugh heartily, but anyone who happened to hear them was irresistibly affected by laughter too.

4. Eisenach – view of the town c.1650.

This, then, is the general picture of the Bach family as it developed through the generations: initially concentrated in Thuringia, building up a strong tradition of professional

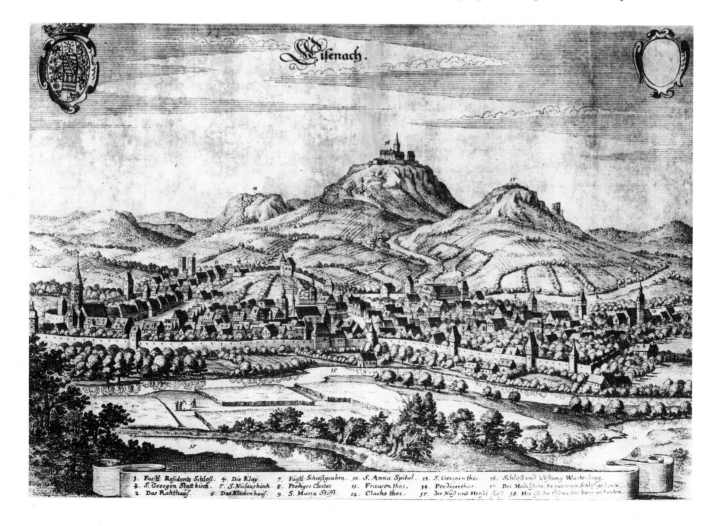

5. Eisenach – the old town-pipers' tower as it is today.

musicianship, firmly integrated in the provincial bourgeois movement which had its origins among the common people, and possessing a marked degree of family unity. These are all features that were still present in the lifetime of Johann Sebastian Bach.

6. The Wartburg near Eisenach.

Childhood and Youth

Since the middle of the seventeenth century, when Merian published his engravings of Eisenach in his topography, little had changed. The town, with its town-hall, the Church of St George and the ducal palace at its centre, lay, surrounded by a protective wall, in the shadow of the Wartburg which loomed not only high above it but well outside the confines of the town. The population had remained at about 7000 and the citizens' lives were determined by artisan traditions and the presence of the ducal court.

Like many other comparable towns, Eisenach had at its disposal considerable musical forces of an individuality brought about through the constant interaction of town and court traditions. The most prominent position among these forces was occupied by the court orchestra, the Duchy of Eisenach being typical of the innumerable tiny but independent states whose ruler regarded music as a useful means of self-aggrandizement.

The court employed only a modest number of musicians (additional forces being brought in from the town and the surrounding district for special occasions) but among them were some redoubtable personalities. Johann Pachelbel was the court organist and a member of the court orchestra from 1677 to 1678; Daniel Eberlein held the post of *Hofkapellmeister* from 1685 until 1692; and, from 1708 to 1712 this post was filled by Georg Philipp Telemann, who also led the orchestra. As was the practice at that time, many members of the court orchestra also performed extra-musical duties in the treasury, for instance, or in the running of the household. One of these dual-purpose functionaries at the court of the Duke of Eisenach was Johann Ambrosius Bach.

The cultivation of music in the town and in the church was closely interwoven, both coming under the direction of the organist and choirmaster. In Eisenach the choir consisted of pupils in the Latin School whose duties included the provision of music for special occasions. The compensation for these special services provided an important source of income for the young choristers. One of the most outstanding men ever to have charge of church music in Eisenach was Johann Christoph Bach (1642–1703). Born in Arnstadt, he was a member of the Wechmar branch of the family. After working for two years as an organist in his home town, he was appointed town organist in Eisenach in 1665. Besides playing the organ in St George's Church, he also performed at court on both the organ and harpsichord. In addition, he was greatly respected as a composer, and was referred to by Johann Sebastian's family many decades later as "the great expressive composer". His motets, early examples of the German form, are certainly among the most impressive and most elaborately worked of their time, and it was by his detailed study of these works that the young Johann Sebastian was to forge a strong link

7. The Wartburg
c.1690.

8. Eisenach –
St George's Church,
where Johann
Sebastian Bach was
baptized.

with the German motet tradition of the seventeenth century. Even when he was Cantor in Leipzig he was still revising and performing his uncle's compositions.

The profession of "town musician" in Eisenach had developed from the role of the watchman, whose job it was to signal the hour, sound the alarm in case of fire, and generally alert the citizenry to any event of particular importance. When these duties gradually became more and more involved with music, the position of "town piper" came into being, that designation then becoming "musician to the council". The council musicians formed their own guild, gave each other mutual support, and worked to maintain the standing of their profession.

Johann Ambrosius Bach came to Eisenach in 1671 to take up an appointment of this kind, having held a similar one in Erfurt. Already a greatly respected musician, he became the principal figure in the musical life of Eisenach and remained so until his death in 1695. In his contract with the town council it stipulated that he should

9. Eisenach – No. 11, Rittergasse, Johann Ambrosius Bach's house from 1671 to 1673.

10. Johann Ambrosius Bach.

. . . perform his duties in a fitting manner and should, together with four other persons, make his services available as herein set forth: Twice every day at the Town Hall, in the forenoon at 10 o'clock and in the evening at 5 o'clock, he shall blow a signal, and this he shall do in the manner which has become customary. He shall also present himself at Divine Service on all feast days and every Sunday, at the morning and evening service before and after the sermon as the cantor shall require.

He had ample opportunity to augment his income by performing at private functions such as weddings, christenings, funerals, birthday celebrations, and guild anniversaries.

In these lucrative fields the town pipers had to fend off — not always successfully — the rivalry of the humbler, often itinerant fiddlers.

The appearance of Johann Ambrosius Bach is known to us through a portrait probably executed by Johann David Herlicius. He portrays him unconventionally, with no wig, no court suit, but casually posed and looking the observer straight in the eye; behind him is an open window through which we can glimpse the Wartburg. It is the portrait of a self-assured citizen, a man well aware of his abilities and with no reason to hide his light under a bushel. His very commission of a portrait of this kind expresses his assurance and

11. Entry for Johann Sebastian Bach's baptism, 23.3.1685.

his position as a respected member of the community; it is almost unique among late-seventeenth-century portraits of musicians.

Johann Sebastian Bach was the eighth and last child of his parents, who, in 1685 (the year of his birth), were in the very prime of life. The family home was in the Rittergasse, and Johann Sebastian spent the first ten years of his life here surrounded by the music not only of his father, which now centred principally around the violin and trumpet, but that of the numerous relatives who came to visit them from far and near. His world also included the modest life of the municipality and eventually that of the Latin School, which he attended from 1693 until 1695. The school register for 1695 shows that Johann Sebastian was absent on 103 occasions. This was due to the terrible tragedy suffered by the family when both parents died within nine months of each other. His mother, Elisabeth, died in May 1694 and his father in February of the following year. Although Johann Ambrosius had remarried in the November following Elisabeth's death, a stepmother of only three months' standing can have been little more than a stranger to the children. Johann Sebastian's childhood in Eisenach had thus come to an abrupt end, but this first decade was to prove the foundation-stone for his whole career. His involvement with music was already established as were his links with the family: these were the raw materials with which, upon that foundation, his entire future could be built.

His eldest brother, Johann Christoph (1671–1721), who bore the same name as their uncle in Eisenach, had been living in Ohrdruf since 1690, having already served as organist in Erfurt and Arnstadt, and it was into his household that the two younger brothers, Johann Jakob and Johann Sebastian, were received. Here at least their education could be continued in the bosom of the family. The two boys probably left Eisenach very shortly after the death of their father. Johann Sebastian's name appears in the registers of the Ohrdruf Lyceum from 1696 until 1699. His school records show that he was an exceptional pupil who progressed from *tertia* to *prima* (fourth to sixth form) in a shorter period than usual and excelled in a class where the other pupils were two or three years older than he was.

Johann Christoph had connections both within the family and with professional colleagues outside it. He had studied with Johann Pachelbel in Erfurt and acquired an excellent reputation as an organist and harpsichordist. In the Ohrdruf church register we find him glowingly referred to as "optimus artifex" (an excellent musician). Teaching in school, which he was also required to do, gave him rather less pleasure; he avoided it whenever possible. Where the musical education of his youngest brother was concerned, however, he seems to have provided strict and regular instruction, building firmly upon the foundations that had already been laid during the Eisenach years. The young Johann Sebastian can surely not have lacked for stimulus to his musical development in Ohrdruf. The Lyceum curriculum, which embraced both classical and orthodox Protestant subjects, and the steady evolution of his musical skills and abilities, combined to develop the personality of the young man. A reliable singer, he became a member of the *chorus musicus*. Many of the acquaintances and friends that he made in Ohrdruf were later to be of importance to Johann Sebastian in his career. One of these was his schoolfriend Georg

*12. Ohrdruf –
St Michael's Church,
gutted by fire in
1753, destroyed in
World War II.*

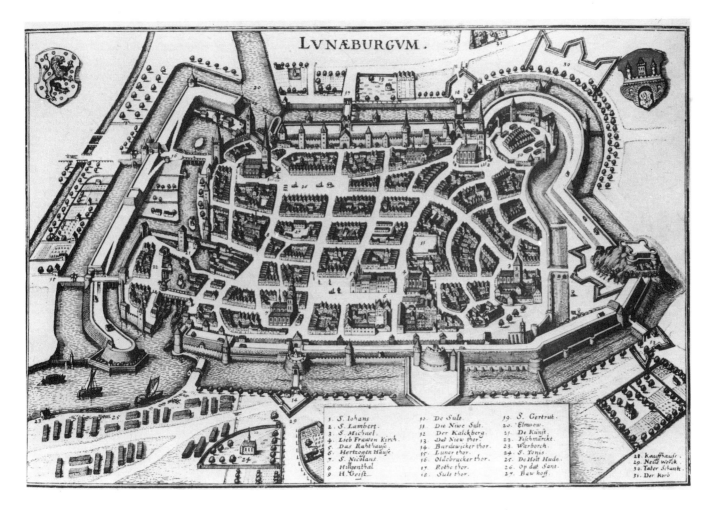

LVNÆBVRGVM.

1. S. Iohans	10. De Sult	19. S. Gertrut.
2. S. Lambert.	11. Die Niwe Sult.	20. Elmouw.
3. S. Michael.	12. Der Kalckberg.	21. De Kunst.
4. Lieb Frawen Kirch	13. Dat Niew thor	22. Fischmarckt.
5. Das Rahthause	14. Bardewicker thor	23. Warborch.
6. Hertzogen Häuse	15. Luner thor.	24. S. Tonis
7. S. Nicolaus	16. Oldebrucker thor.	25. De Holt Hude.
8. Hilgenthal	17. Rothe thor.	26. Op dat Sant.
9. H. Geist.	18. Sult thor.	27. Bauhoff.
		28. Kauffhause
		29. Neue Werck
		30. Tater Schank
		31. Der Korb

Erdmann, with whom he left Ohrdruf on 15 March 1700. The two boys were bound for Lüneburg where they enrolled as trebles in the Matins choir attached to the Church of St Michael. They had probably been recommended to this choir by Elias Herda, a former Cantor in Ohrdruf.

13. Lüneburg – town plan c.1654.

In the ancient Hanseatic town of Lüneburg, the *chorus symphonicus* and the smaller but more select Matins choir had, together with a succession of instrumentalists, developed the capacity for elaborate and sophisticated performances of church music. The town could also boast some outstanding organists, among whom the most eminent was Georg Böhm (1661–1733) of the neighbouring Johanniskirche, who had been born in Hohenkirchen near Ohrdruf and came to Lüneburg from Hamburg in 1698. It seems likely that Johann Sebastian received lessons from him both in organ playing and general musicianship.

The young Johann Sebastian was an eager participant in the active musical life of the church. He must have welcomed the opportunity to become familiar with many of the works of renowned masters which had been unknown to him before, and he had at his disposal the richly stocked library of the Michaeliskirche where, among the works of other famous German cantors, he would have found those of Heinrich and Johann Christoph Bach. The cantor of the Michaeliskirche, who was also in charge of the library, was at that time a fellow Thuringian, Emanuel Praetorius.

Bach was now in his adolescence. His ever-increasing knowledge and experience and his fast-developing skills had earned him the respect of his teachers and fellow choristers and strengthened his own self-confidence. But this was not enough:

From time to time he would travel from Lüneburg to Hamburg to hear the organist at the Catharinenkirche, Jan Adams Reinken, who was one of the most celebrated organists of the day. Here, on several occasions, he also had the chance to listen to the famous orchestra employed by the Duke of Celle, which was largely composed of Frenchmen and played in the French style that was something quite new at that

14. Celle – the palace.

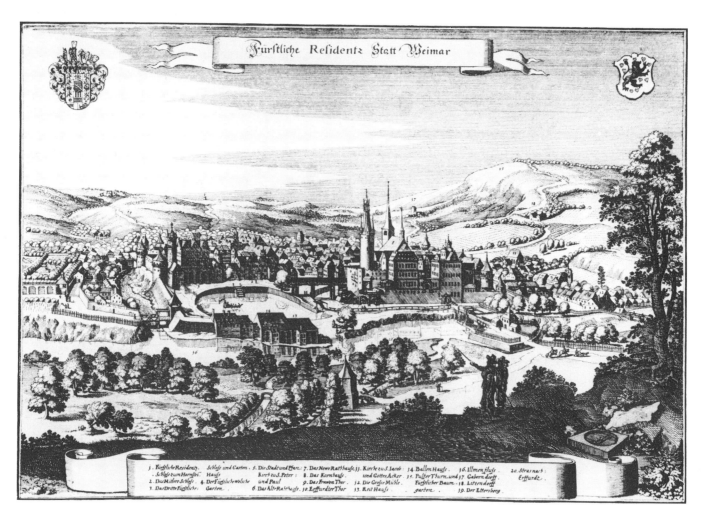

15. Weimar – view of the town c.1650.

time and in that part of the country and provided him with his first opportunity to learn about French taste.[1]

Bach later made the acquaintance of the elderly Reinken, and he committed the distinctive features of the French style and the sound of the string orchestra firmly to memory. In every way his musical experience was deepened and enriched during these three years, so much so that Lüneburg could well be described as his musical university. But his time there was to be limited. Once his voice had broken he could no longer sing in the choir and was obliged to seek employment elsewhere. In the summer of 1702 he had already successfully competed for the post of organist at St Jacob's Church in Sanger-hausen, but the Duke Johann Georg of Saxe-Weissenfels intervened and the post was offered to someone else.

Because of the Bach family's musical connections all over central Germany, it is natural to assume that, when it came to finding a position for the eighteen-year-old Johann Sebastian, the family would help. But we know nothing about his departure from Lüneburg except that by March 1703 he was a paid musician at the court of Duke Johann Ernst of Saxe-Weimar. This, however, lasted only until September of the same year and affected his career very little.

16. Arnstadt – Bach Church, formerly the New Church. View of the organ gallery.

Organist in Arnstadt and Mühlhausen

In October of 1699, when Johann Sebastian was still living with his eldest brother in Ohrdruf, the town council of Arnstadt commissioned an organ for their new church. By the summer of 1703 the instrument was completed and in July the council officially approved the work following its inspection by the Arnstadt organist, Johann Georg Kallenberg, and, despite his youth, the fledgling court musician Johann Sebastian Bach. Johann Sebastian's invitation would doubtless never have been issued had it not been for the well-established reputation of the Arnstadt Bachs, but evidently his own skill impressed the authorities as well, and a month later he was installed as organist in the new church of Arnstadt. This is indeed proof of his outstanding abilities both as an organist and harpsichord player. Bach himself must have viewed his appointment as a definite step in the right direction, which is proved both by the speed with which he left Weimar for Arnstadt and by the fact that in securing such a post he was subscribing to the time-honoured family tradition.

His contract of employment was drawn up on 9 August 1703, and sets out his duties in some detail: "In his post, profession, practice and knowledge to show industry and dedication", it read, and further stipulates that he should be punctual in his attendances for services on Sundays and feast-days and other occasions, and that he should "treat [the organ] properly, take good care of it and be fully responsible for it". As was customary at that time, even general rules of conduct were specified. His salary was remarkably good. The money came partly from a tax on beer, partly from collections taken in church, and partly from profits made by the hospital. The size of his salary is an indication of the high esteem in which the council held him. The New Church had been dedicated in 1683; the completion of the organ in 1703 provided the final touch to the building. Arnstadt was then a town of some 3800 inhabitants and an important trading centre for the region bordering the forest of Thuringia. There was a strong bourgeois element and many opportunities for the young organist to mix with men who could stimulate and inspire him. At this time, Johann Sebastian probably lived at "The Golden Crown", an inn owned by one Martin Feldhaus, a relative and the mayor of the town.

Count Anton Günther von Schwarzburg lived in a palace in Arnstadt, Schloss Neidecksburg. He employed an orchestra of some twenty musicians, and as this had to be supplemented on certain occasions, it is reasonable to assume that he called on the young Bach more than once. Although his contract of employment makes no specific mention of it, one of the New Church organist's duties was to rehearse the choir in new pieces. In performance, the prefect conducted, the organist accompanied. Bach's work with this choir brought him little pleasure, however, for the schoolboys, some of whom were older than him, were undisciplined and their standard of performance was probably pitifully low. Concentrated work must have been almost an impossibility, and the organist's outbursts of temper cannot have improved matters at all. In spite of attempts on the part of the Consistory to impose some sort of control on the choir by repeated reprimands, the situation worsened until, on the evening of 4 August 1705, it erupted in a street brawl initiated by the Geyersbach schoolboys in which Bach appears to have played anything but a passive role. At his suggestion there were further discussions with the Consistory, but his work with the choir ceased completely.

In spite of the drawbacks, Bach's duties as organist gave him plenty of opportunity to practise on the instrument and devote himself to his art. All in all, it would seem that the three years he spent in Lüneburg, too, where he made so many valuable contacts in North German musical circles, had made a favourable impression on him. Besides Lüneburg, Hamburg and Celle there was one other musically important town that he had not yet visited: Lübeck, where the great Dietrich Buxtehude was organist at the Marienkirche which had an exceptional tradition of music. Bach was still most anxious to hear him and to get to know his work. At the end of October 1705 he obtained four weeks' leave from the Consistory and set off for Lübeck leaving his cousin Johann Ernst (1683–1739) as his deputy.

Four weeks was an absurdly unrealistic time allowance for such an expedition. Lübeck was a long way from Arnstadt and the young man, according to the *Nekrolog*, made the journey on foot. Returning north must have revived many memories of Lüne-

17. Arnstadt – panoramic view.

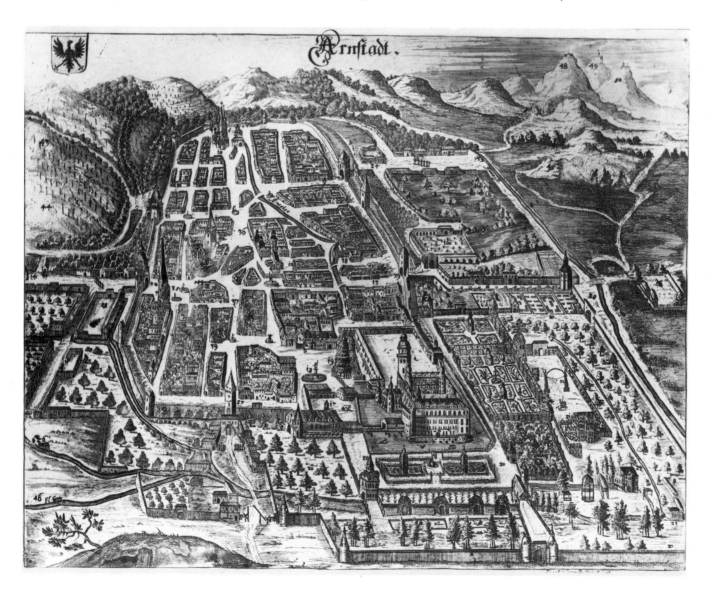

burg, but the factor of prime importance was that the sixty-eight-year-old Buxtehude
was a leading authority on church music. The four weeks became three months. Bach
must have been very deeply impressed by Buxtehude and by the quality of music
associated with St Mary's. Above all, he enjoyed the famous "Abendmusiken", or
musical evenings, organized and conducted by Buxtehude. The admiration was mutual,
moreover; had Bach been willing to marry the old man's daughter as custom required, he
could have succeeded him in his post.

On his return to Arnstadt, however, he found that his extended leave of absence had
not endeared him to his employers. He was summoned before the Consistory on
21 February 1706 and defended himself in a brief and rather surprising way. He trusted,
he said, that his deputy had acquitted himself well and given no cause for complaint! The
Consistory, however, took the opportunity of complaining about other things, particularly concerning Bach's fulfilment of his duties. He had, they said, "introduced many

*19. Arnstadt – Bach
Church.*

strange variations during the congregational hymns and extra notes which confused the
congregation. . . . And also, it is disturbing that none of his own compositions have been
performed on account of his unwillingness to establish a good relationship with the
students; thus, would he please explain whether he would be willing to perform Figured
as well as Choral music with the students?''

    This last question was a pointed reference to the tension that existed between Bach
and his recalcitrant choir, a tension that persisted even after further discussions. The
reproach of having introduced "strange variations" went deeper. Bach's style of organ
playing was at variance with the accepted norms: his treatment of the chorale was freer,
the "strange variations" and "extra notes" were, presumably, part and parcel of that
heightened poetic feeling that we find in the Chorale Preludes and which give us such
insight into his musical thought-processes. That this development was already clearly in
evidence during the Arnstadt period is beyond dispute, and further reference will be
made to this. Later in the same year (on 11 November) Bach was again summoned before
the Consistory. After being admonished roundly yet again for his failure to achieve a
good working relationship with the choir, he was asked a delicate question: Why had he
allowed a strange young woman access to the organ loft to sing? Bach replied that he had
informed Pastor Uthe (the minister at the New Church) of his intention to do so. But it
was still not general practice at this time for women to be allowed to sing in church. This
strange young woman, however, must have been Johann Sebastian's cousin, Maria Barbara
Bach, the daughter of Johann Michael Bach, organist at Gehren. One year later she was

to become Johann Sebastian's first wife.

Bach's work as a composer really began during the years in Arnstadt, and became ever more varied. Lüneburg had, of course, seen the birth of his earliest surviving compositions, but it was here in Arnstadt, working as a professional organist, that he produced his first mature compositions.

That works for the organ predominate is hardly surprising, since, as a proficient organist, he was able to perform his own compositions. We might mention first the group of organ chorales, whose unconventional harmonization goes a long way to explaining the nervous reaction of a Consistory unwilling to subject the congregation to any shock. The arrangement of chorales for the organ dates back to Bach's time in Lüneburg, when he was influenced by Reinken, Böhm and Pachelbel. His virtuosic powers, too, had been strengthened during the time he spent in Lübeck with Buxtehude. The organ fugue, the combination of prelude and fugue and the fantasia were the forms which then predominated. Even as early as this period in Arnstadt, Bach was producing works that testify to his brilliance as a performer, and reveal a composer of unfettered power and bold imagination. What is perhaps the most famous and most widely-played of all Bach's works for the organ, the Toccata and Fugue in D minor (BWV 565), was apparently conceived in Arnstadt.

Beside compositions for the organ, Bach also wrote a quantity of harpsichord music. The Capriccio in E major (BWV 993) was written in honour of Johann Sebastian's eldest brother, Johann Christoph, and that in B flat major (BWV 992) commemorated "the departure of his well-beloved brother" Johann Jacob for Sweden. In 1704, the brother with whom Johann Sebastian had left Ohrdruf following their parents' deaths, was leaving his Thuringian homeland to enter the service of the King of Sweden as a soldier. He was to experience the danger and turmoil of war for many years and to die, in 1722, as a member of the Swedish court orchestra. The B flat major Capriccio which Johann Sebastian wrote for him, translates his affection for his brother into playful music. Contrary to previously-held opinion, however, there are no grounds for assuming that any of Bach's extant cantatas should be included among the Arnstadt compositions.

The hearings before the Consistory made it clear that, although no one was prepared to take decisive action against him, the people of Arnstadt objected to the way their

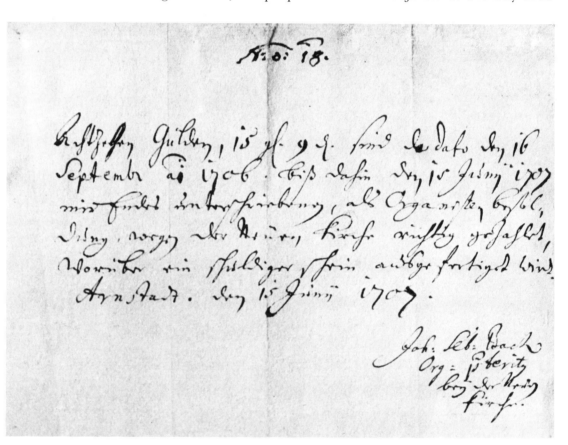

21. Johann Sebastian Bach's salary receipt, Arnstadt, 15.6.1707.

organist was carrying out his duties. In turn, Bach failed to see why he should suppress his musical creativeness for their sake or why he should waste his time on an incompetent choir. Realizing that the time had come to strike out in a new direction, he began the search for another post, possibly with marriage plans making the decision even more imperative.

In the Free Imperial City of Mühlhausen, situated in the Thuringian basin, Johann Georg Ahle (*b.* 1651) had died on 5 December 1706. One of the most important musicians in Thuringia, he had succeeded his father as organist at St Blasius' Church in 1673 and had held it ever since. Various renowned musicians had given the city a special reputation, but it had once been, during the Peasant War, the seat of the "eternal council" that sat under Thomas Müntzer and so had been a centre of early bourgeois revolution in Germany. The vacancy in Mühlhausen must have seemed to Bach a good opportunity to escape from the unpleasantness and problems in Arnstadt, and he went for an audition early in 1707; on the strength of this, the council decided on 24 May that "Herr Pach [*sic*] of Arnstadt" should be employed and an "equitable agreement worked out with him". On 14 June the matter was discussed with Bach himself and the following day he was installed as organist at the St Blasius' Church. His salary was higher than Ahle's; it

equalled that which he had been paid in Arnstadt and was supplemented, in accordance with local tradition, by an allowance of corn, logs, and brushwood.[2] Four members of the council were unable to sign the agreement but gave their approval orally, for, like many others, they had suffered from the effects of a terrible fire which had reduced over 360 houses in the city to dust and ashes on 30 May. The church had escaped, but the conditions for church music can hardly have been improved by the disaster. On 29 June — the day after he received his salary for the last quarter — Bach informed the Arnstadt council of his contract at Mühlhausen, returned the key of the organ loft, and tendered his resignation.

Bach was not without personal connections in Mühlhausen. Johann Hermann Bellstadt, a town councillor and scribe, was related by marriage to the Bachs of Arnstadt, and Johann Friedrich Wender, who built the organ in Arnstadt's Neukirche, was living in the town. In the autumn Bach married Maria Barbara Bach, the "strange young woman" about whose presence in the organ loft he had been questioned by the Consistory the year before. The banns were read in Arnstadt on 2 October, and the marriage took place in the church of Dornheim, a village close by. The relevant entry in the church register reads:

On 17 October 1707 the worthy Johann Sebastian Bach, bachelor, organist of the Church of Divi Blasii, Mühlhausen, lawfully begotten son of the deceased honourable and distinguished Ambrosius Bach, town organist and musician of Eisenach, to the virtuous Maria Barbara, youngest surviving daughter of the late right worthy and distinguished Michael Bach, organist at Gehren, here in the house of God, by permission of his Lordship the Count, and after banns duly called at Arnstadt, were joined in marriage.

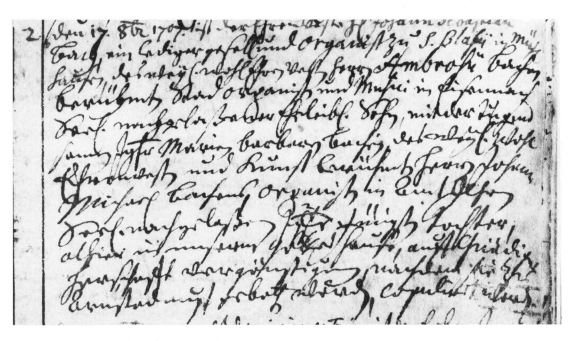

23. *Entry for the marriage of Johann Sebastian and Maria Barbara Bach, 17.10.1707.*

Shortly before his marriage Bach's financial position had been improved by a legacy of fifty gulden from his mother's uncle, Tobias Lämmerhirt of Erfurt.

The "Wedding Quodlibet" (BWV 524) with words by the headmaster of the school in Arnstadt, Johann Friedrich Treiber, and which survives only as a fragment, is probably connected with Bach's marriage ceremony. The manuscript version that we have is probably a re-working of the original song, which would have been a robust and jovial improvisation — just the sort of piece, in fact, that we know the Bach family enjoyed at their gatherings.

On 4 February 1708 Bach directed a performance of his cantata *Gott ist mein König* ("God is my King", BWV 71) in the imposing Marienkirche at Mühlhausen on the occasion of the town council's re-election. This work is not only a high point among his compositions in Mühlhausen, but signals a new activity for him: writing cantatas. That the work attracted an unusual amount of attention and made a significant impact may be inferred from the fact that the parts as well as the text were printed at the expense of the council. It was to remain the only one of his cantatas that Bach ever saw in print. The scale of the work is imposing, the forces lavish: three trumpets, timpani, two oboes, recorders, bassoon, strings, organ, four solo singers and a four-part choir. This bold conception reveals the twenty-three-year-old Bach already well on his way towards the achievements of a master.

Bach was not destined to remain long at Mühlhausen, however. In the spring of his arrival there he was already putting out feelers towards Weimar once again. Although he was undoubtedly extremely busy at Mühlhausen, and in spite of the fact that he had taken the post on a long-term basis, his work there came to an end in a surprisingly short

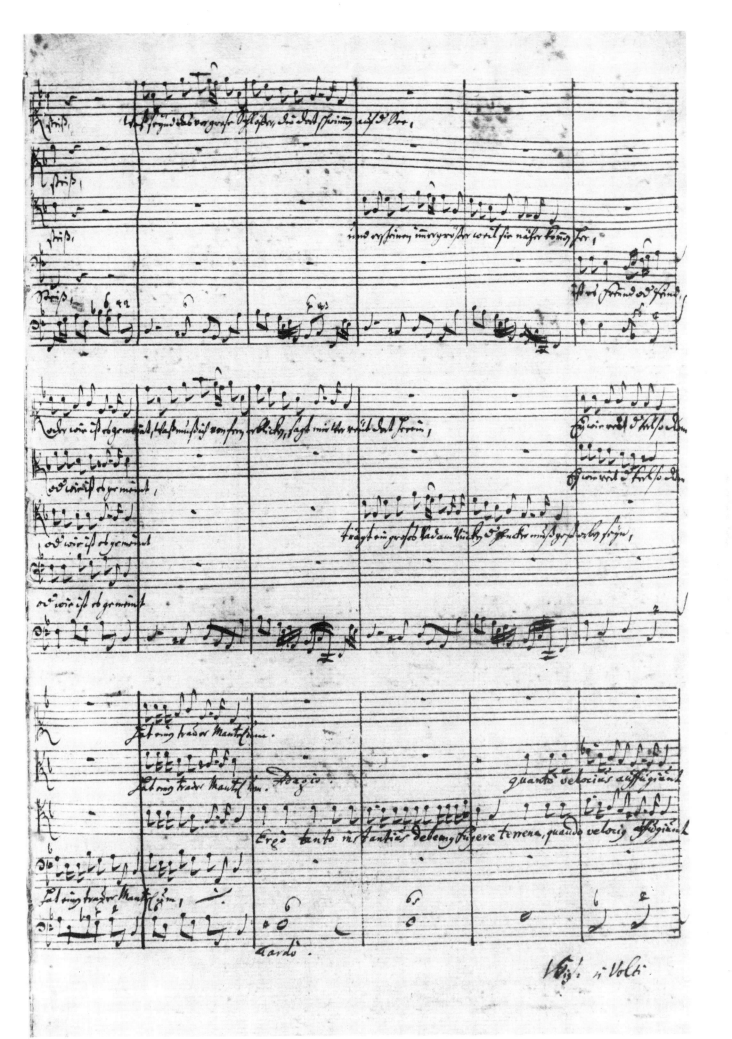

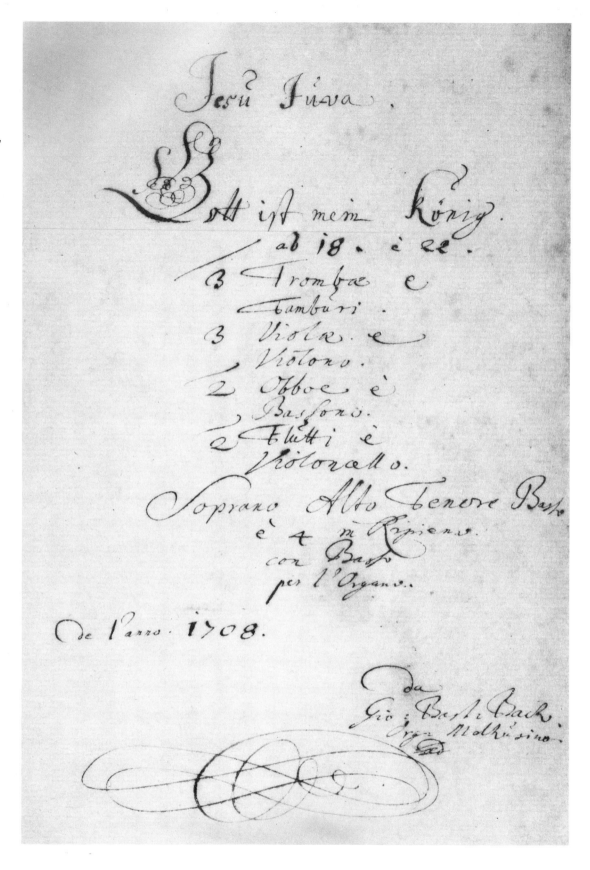

26. *"Gott ist mein König", BWV 71, cantata for the re-election of Mühlhausen council, 1708 – title page of the autograph score.*

time. Immediately after the performance of the cantata just mentioned, Bach put forward proposals for the modification of the organ in St Blasius' Church. This remains one of the most informative documents we have about Bach's ideas on organs, and reveals his extensive knowledge about their construction. The modifications were not, however, completed before Bach left Mühlhausen. Another reason that we can assume that Bach originally intended to make his stay in Mühlhausen a long one is that he was at pains to create and collect the widest possible repertoire for performance there. He was affected, however, by conflicts within the church between the orthodox Lutherans and the Pietists who, in their search for a more deeply emotional form of worship, were strongly opposed to the use of any but the most simple music in church. The points at issue between the two factions would be difficult to clarify, but it was the Lutheran tradition to which Bach and his family adhered, and, indeed, it would have been strange for any musician to have sympathized to any great degree with the Pietists. In Mühlhausen the orthodox faction had its champion in the person of Pastor Christian Eilmahr of the Marienkirche, while the Blasiuskirche was the Pietist stronghold on account of the views of its pastor, Johann Adolf Frohne. Conflicts of this sort, which did not make the work of the organist easier, were not peculiar to Mühlhausen; Bach was to encounter them again and again throughout his career in church music. But they were probably not the main reason he decided to leave the city. Rather, his decision seems to have been influenced by the general situation that prevailed and not least by the question of an adequate salary, for financial responsibilities were now weighing on the young organist with a wife to support and a household to maintain.

In June 1708 modifications to the organ of the Court chapel in Weimar were completed; moreover, the court organist, the greatly-respected Johann Effler, was about to retire. On 5 June Bach and his wife travelled to Dornheim to attend a wedding in the church where they themselves had been married. The groom was the minister who had married them, the bride was an aunt of Maria Barbara's. It seems probable that Bach took this opportunity to re-establish contact with the court at Weimar. At any rate, it was later in the same month (on the 25th) that he submitted his letter of resignation to the parochial council in Mühlhausen, giving as his reason the Weimar appointment. Thus, in just a few months — maybe only weeks — the idea of such a change had been born and the decision made and acted upon without hesitation. This ability to assess his professional circumstances and to change them radically when necessary was to remain with him throughout his life and to become very useful again later on.

Bach's letter of resignation from his post in Mühlhausen is the oldest important authentic document in Bach's own hand that has come down to us.[3] In it he explains his position in detail and describes the conditions under which he worked in Mühlhausen and his concern for ". . . Church music so performed as to exalt the glory of God". He also mentions the limitations he experienced there in comparison to those found in other places, his "select collection of choice pieces of sacred music", and sets out his suggestions for the modifications to be made to the faulty organ. In conclusion he admits to financial pressures; his circumstances are such, he says, that he has "not enough to live on", and this weighs heavily upon him as a newly-married man. But, he continues, an opportunity, albeit unforeseen, had arisen in that "His Serene Highness the Duke of Saxe-Weimar has graciously admitted me into his Court and Chamber Orchestras".

Thus, after barely one year, Bach left his post in Mühlhausen.

27. Weimar –
Wilhelmsburg Palace,
the so-called Bastille
and tower.

Service in the Courts of Weimar and Cöthen

In the early eighteenth century German music was characterized by the simultaneous existence of two disparate and highly elaborate traditions: the music of the court and that of the town. In Arnstadt and Mühlhausen Bach had been in the service of the town, his posts as organist subject to those conditions of municipal music with which he had been familiar since his childhood in Eisenach. In the urban community — as we have already seen in the case of Ambrosius Bach — sacred and secular music were closely linked. In the church, the music provided for the services and for the embellishment of all the other occasions such as weddings, funerals and feast-days became the artistic manifestation of religious practice. In the secular sphere, music served for edification and entertainment, for social activities and dancing, and also added pomp and circumstance to civic ceremonies. The music produced to satisfy aristocratic taste differed in quality from that produced for the townspeople. Both court and town used music on similar occasions, sacred and secular; but the style naturally differed and so did the forces available, at least to some degree. Indeed, the middle class had by now developed sufficient financial independence from the courts to be in a position to employ and commission the means for its own cultural life. But in spite of the growing economic power of the bourgeoisie, the courts remained the true centres of political power and there was as yet no way that the middle classes could challenge this in Germany — unlike England and Holland.

At the courts, however, the cultivation and development of all the arts, including music, still depended on the skills of the ordinary people employed there. The cultured image that was so prized in aristocratic circles depended for its very existence on the common people, on the craftsmen and musicians from burgher families who worked there as composers, *Kapellmeister*, instrumentalists, and singers. The cross-influences created by this daily association of middle-class skills with the artistic life at court were extraordinarily strong in the early eighteenth century.

The flow of musicians between court and municipal posts was continual. More and more, musicians tended to seek civic employment in order to avoid being subjected to the arbitrary and dictatorial orders of some absolute ruler. Johann Beer, the leader of the court orchestra at Weissenfels, described the situation in his *Discourses on Music* (1719) thus:

> The republics pride themselves generally on retaining the loyalty of their servants better than the courts, and when I consider that in the case of the former there are many people at the head, while in the case of the latter there is only one, such a view is easily maintained . . . It follows from this that many court musicians yearn for the town . . .

Bach had become acquainted with the conditions of court service during his first brief appointment at Weimar in 1703; he had also experienced it in Arnstadt. Now, in Weimar, began a period of nearly fifteen years' unbroken service at court. Later he still maintained links with court music, though to a lesser degree. His whole professional and artistic development vividly demonstrates the inter-relationship between municipal and court music, with Bach always working from the standpoint of his bourgeois heritage and cast of mind.

The Duchy of Saxe-Weimar, with its seat of government in Weimar itself, was one of many small German states that had no far-reaching political importance. In no way could Weimar compete with Berlin (Prussia) or Dresden (Saxony) — to name but two obvious examples — in political, economic, or military terms. Duke Wilhelm Ernst, the head of state, was on bad terms with his nephew Ernst August, who, although officially co-regent, had no real influence in the political sphere. While Duke Wilhelm's marriage had been childless and had ended in divorce, his nephew had two sons. Ernst August's half-brother, Prince Johann Ernst, possessed a remarkable talent for music, but he died in 1715 at the age of nineteen. The religious zeal with which Duke Wilhelm Ernst ruled was perhaps not unrelated to his unhappy personal situation. The importance that he attributed to the education of his people and the interest that he displayed in the arts were both untypical of the time in which he lived. During his regency the court orchestra was enlarged and improved. In 1698, for example, he summoned Paul von Westhoff (1656–1705), a highly-esteemed violin virtuoso, composer and teacher to Weimar; and two years before, he had established an opera house at Schloss Wilhelmsburg on the banks of the River Ilm not far from the centre of town that made Weimar into one of the few places that concerned itself with German opera.

Bach's first appointment in Weimar, in the spring of 1703, had been as a violinist in the private orchestra of the younger brother, Duke Johann Ernst, whose residence was in the "Red Palace". His second appointment, confirmed sometime before 25 June 1708, was as chamber musician and court organist to Duke Wilhelm Ernst, succeeding Johann Effler. The dual appointment meant a considerable widening of his professional capacity.

28. Weimar – view of the town.

Der Durchlauchtigste Fürste und Herr, Herr Wilhelm Ernst, Hertzog zu Sachsen,
Jülich, Cleve und Bergen auch Engern und Westphalen, Landgraf in Thüringen, Marckgraf zu
Meißen gefürsteter Graf zu Henneberg, Graf zu der Marck und Ravensberg, Herr zu Ravenst...

Der hohen Sachsen zier der Schmuck Durchlauchter welt
Wird hier von Künstlers hand im Schatten vorgestellt o
Doch sieht man Gottes bild auß seiner Seele strahlen,
Und seinen Himmel geist sich selbst durch Leben mahlen.

Ernst August
Herzog zu Sachsen Weymar Eisenach
und Jena, Kayserl: General der Cavallerie

The organ was situated in a loft above the palace chapel, and, during the services, the singers and instrumentalists performed from there. The organ-loft was connected to the chapel below by an elaborately-worked opening (which could be closed if so desired) so the music floated down from heaven, as it were, into the "Heavenly City" as the chapel had been dubbed. The space in the organ-loft provided the necessary space for the organ, the orchestra and the choir, and this is where Bach and his fellow musicians worked. Bach's contract of employment no longer exists, and we do not know when or even if he auditioned on the recently-repaired organ in the chapel, but domestic accounts inform us that he received payment towards the expenses of the move from Mühlhausen to Weimar on 14 July 1708, and that his annual salary was more than that of his predecessor. In addition he received four cords of fire-wood. From the start, Bach was considerably better off in Weimar than he had been in Mühlhausen, and his income constantly increased over the years. In addition, he received quarterly bonuses in lieu of the customary payment in kind and from 1715 his supplementary earnings were equivalent to those earned by the Kapellmeister. Thus, within eight years Bach's recorded income in Weimar doubled, a clear indication of the way in which he had consolidated his position and earned an ever-increasing reputation. To be sure, Bach never let an opportunity for financial improvement escape him. As far as we know, Bach's residence in Weimar was at the house of Immanuel Weldig, himself a court musician and master of the pages. The house, which was immediately adjacent to the market place and opposite the Red Palace, was destroyed by bombs in 1945.

The Weimar court orchestra to which Bach belonged numbered, in the years between 1708 and 1717, about fifteen. Some of its members were already known to Bach from his previous appointment. Apart from the regular members, there were about seven drummers and trumpeters who could be called upon for certain occasions. In overall charge of the music as Hofkapellmeister, Johann Samuel Drese had been at Weimar since 1683 and would remain until his death in 1716. In 1707 a new town organist had been appointed. This was Johann Gottfried Walther (1684–1748), a cousin of Johann Sebastian's who had married at about the same time that Bach took up his appointment in Weimar. He had been a pupil of Johann Bernhard Bach in Erfurt, had also taught

31

himself a great deal, and showed a lively interest in both the theory and practice of music. The cousins enjoyed a close professional association and the two families were on very friendly terms, as is evidenced by the fact that Bach became godfather to Walther's son. As both men had an innate curiosity about their art and new developments in it, we may safely assume there was a lively exchange of information. Such association with a fellow organist and composer must have been an important element of Bach's life in Weimar. Walther, and presumably Bach too, also acted as teacher to Prince Johann Ernst, who possessed considerable musical gifts.

31. J. S. Bach, Konzertmeister at Weimar (?), unauthenticated portrait.

32. *Halle – view of the town.*

Weimar, which was at that time a town of some 5000 inhabitants naturally had its town piper too, who, with his colleagues, would occasionally be invited to join the Duke's musicians. As was so often the case, well-trained schoolboy choristers seemed yet again to be in short supply. But the Duke also saw to it that the town musicians did not over-indulge the people's taste for dancing and entertainment generally. In 1696 he even issued a proclamation which forbade the town musicians from providing music for dancing on Sundays and feast-days, since "dancing in the inns and backstreets has become increasingly prevalent and many blasphemous and venal acts have there taken place with excessive drinking and revelling, lewdness and other unseemly manifestations". Naturally, such a prohibition stood little chance of being obeyed for any length of time.

In Weimar Bach was kept very busy at court. During his first years his reputation as an outstanding performer and also as an expert in organ construction became ever more firmly established. His expertise in the latter field was the result of his work with organ builders such as Heinrich Trebs, and was in keeping with what would have been expected of him. Weimar was obviously not the apogee of his own professional ambitions, for in December 1713 we find him making an excursion to Halle, where a new organist was required at the Liebfrauenkirche; there he performed a cantata by way of self-recommendation. The church council, who were seeking a successor to Friedrich Zachow, offered him the post. On 13 December he accepted, but withdrew his candidature a few weeks later and remained in Weimar where his salary was raised for the second time within the year, and where, on 2 March, at the Duke's command, he was appointed Konzertmeister. This meant that his status was "secondary only to that of the Vice-Kapellmeister". He now occupied a position of considerable responsibility among his colleagues, and the post of Hofkapellmeister, which would give him absolute authority over all the music at the court, was within his reach. The motives behind this appointment were probably two-fold: the present Hofkapellmeister's own waning abilities, and recognition of the fact that Bach's accomplishments were so ideal for the job.

His creative abilities had already been displayed in the very effective Birthday Cantata that he had written in February 1713 for Duke Christian of Weissenfels, *Was mir behagt, ist nur die muntre Jagd* ("The merry hunt is my one delight", BWV 208). It was now officially a part of Bach's duties to produce and perform cantatas for the ducal chapel, and within the space of three years he produced a considerable number of them, of which about twenty have survived. They follow in logical development from the cantatas he wrote for Mühlhausen, and have no equal for variety and vitality in the work of other German composers despite the youth of their creator. Of especial importance was Bach's collaboration with those poets who were central to the development of cantata texts. Prominent among these writers were the court poet Salomon Franck and the pastor, Erdmann Neumeister. The latter was responsible for the incorporation of arias and recitatives into German cantatas, a move which resulted in the cantata and the opera ("Dramma per musica") becoming very closely linked, which was of vital importance in Bach's later cantatas. From now on, Bach wrote an average of one cantata a month until the end of 1716; within a few years he had opened up and explored a whole new, rich kingdom as far as this genre was concerned.

Before the cantata became central to his work, Bach had been predominantly a composer of harpsichord and organ works. The shift in emphasis corresponded to the

changing demands that were made on him professionally. In the *Nekrolog* (Bach's obituary) special mention was made of the organ works Bach wrote in Weimar: "Here he also wrote the majority of his organ works." The chorale prelude, which he had already explored in Arnstadt, now found its logical culmination in the *Orgelbüchlein* (the "Little Organ Book"), a collection of organ chorales for the whole church year, planned on a large scale but never completed. This is an early example of Bach's proclivity for making collections of pieces for teaching purposes, or for passing on his knowledge and experience to others. It shows the composer very much in tune with a contemporary cultural trait which was becoming ever more widespread: the tendency to amass knowledge. The Weimar years also saw the composition of a large number of works for the organ intended for recitals: large-scale preludes and fugues, toccatas, fantasias and canzonas. These works are incomparable examples of unfettered virtuosity combined with an entirely new kind of expressiveness of polyphonic texture made luminous by eloquent cantilena, and of extreme harmonic tension; they form a kind of musical self-portrait of a composer whose nature unites two seeming opposites: an infallible instinct for structure and an inexhaustible spontaneity of imagination. The so-called "Erfurt Bach Portrait" (reproduced on p. 32), probably painted around 1715 when he was Konzertmeister, reveals a dynamic, sensitive and confident man.

In Weimar Bach participated in the more adventurous music-making at Johann Ernst's Red Palace (much to the disapproval of Wilhelm Ernst) where he became acquainted with the latest trends in Italian music. The expressive style and concertante technique of Vivaldi and other composers had a great influence on his own future development. From this, he learned the lightness of touch, the elegance, the unforced and natural expression and the relaxed instrumental virtuosity that he would have sought in vain within the German tradition. This was an incalculable gain that was to ripen to a rich harvest in his own work. The first fruits appeared in a series of concerto arrangements that Bach made in 1713–14, probably at the behest of Johann Ernst, of which six were for the organ and sixteen for the harpsichord. All were based on existing concertos, by Vivaldi, Telemann and Prince Johann Ernst, among others.[4] Johann Gottfried Walther also arranged a similar number of concertos of this kind. The harpsichord arrangements that Bach made are forerunners of the original harpsichord works he wrote in Weimar. These, whose forms are still related to the organ works (preludes, toccatas and fugues predominate) are pieces primarily for domestic use, for teaching, and for music-making in the home, for the harpsichord was still regarded first and foremost as a continuo instrument. However, for some decades a change had been making itself felt, and the foundations of a repertoire for the harpsichord as an independent instrument had been laid. From his Weimar years onwards, Bach contributed to this growing repertory, and with him it achieved a new peak of concentration and intensity. As with the organ pieces, Bach's writing for the harpsichord shows him to have been a performer whose abilities were not only far above the norm, but so far above that he caused a positive sensation. In this context we might cite as proof the often-quoted incident of Bach's contest with the Frenchman, Louis Marchand. The *Nekrolog* relates it thus:

The clavier player and organist famous in France, Marchand, had come to Dresden, had let himself be heard by the King with exceptional success, and was so fortunate as to be offered a highly paid post on the Royal service. The Konzertmeister in Dresden at the time, Volumier, wrote to Bach, whose merits were known to him, at Weimar, and invited him to come forthwith to Dresden, in order to engage in a musical contest with the haughty Marchand. Bach willingly accepted the invitation and journeyed to Dresden. Volumier received him with joy and arranged an opportunity for him to hear his opponent first from a place of concealment. Bach thereupon invited Marchand to a contest, in a courteous letter in which he declared himself ready to execute *ex tempore* whatever musical tasks Marchand should set him and, in turn, expressed his expectation that Marchand would show the same willingness — certainly a proof of great daring. Marchand showed himself quite ready to accept the invitation. The time and place were set, with the foreknowledge of the King. Bach appeared at the appointed time at the scene of the contest, in the home of a leading minister of state, where a large company of persons of high rank and of both sexes was assembled. There was a long wait for Marchand. Finally, the host sent to Marchand's quarters to remind him, in case he should have forgotten, that it was

34. "Der Tag, der ist so freudenreich", BWV 605 – from the autograph of the Orgelbüchlein.

now time to show himself a man. But it was learned, to the great astonishment of everyone, that Monsieur Marchand had, very early in the morning of that same day, left Dresden by express coach. Bach, who thus remained sole master of the scene of the contest, accordingly had plentiful opportunity to exhibit the talents with which he was armed against his opponent. And this he did, to the astonishment of all present. The King had intended to present him on this occasion with 500 thalers; but through the dishonesty of a certain servant, who believed that he could use the gift to better advantage, he was deprived of it, and had to take back with him, as the sole reward of his efforts, the honour he had won.[5]

Throughout Bach's lifetime, this episode served as a vivid proof to his contemporaries of his supremacy as a performer. The occasion was also, in all probability, the beginning of Bach's contact with Dresden, where the excellence of the court music would continue to excite his interest up until his last years in Leipzig.

During his Weimar years, Bach enjoyed a steadily widening circle of acquaintances. Within the town and in places such as Weissenfels, Halle and Dresden, he met musicians who had previously only been names to him and who added greatly to his professional experience. His family, too, was growing. Between 1708 and 1715 Maria Barbara gave birth to six children. A set of twins died shortly after their birth in 1713, but three of the sons born in Weimar survived and became exceptional musicians: Wilhelm Friedemann (born 22 November 1710), Carl Philipp Emanuel (born 8 March 1714) and Johann Gottfried Bernhard (born 11 May 1715). The rapid increase in the size of his family meant that Bach was constantly seeking ways to increase his income — all the more so after the experience in Dresden, which showed him that financial reward did not always follow professional success. So the occasional invitation to test an organ, for example, not only gave him an opportunity for demonstrating his knowledge and skill, but also provided him with welcome additions to his income.

On 1 December 1716 the Weimar Court Kapellmeister, Johann Samuel Drese, died. Bach had every reason to hope he would be offered the position on the strength of his record as a successful and versatile composer and Konzertmeister. However, the post was first offered to Georg Philipp Telemann who concurrently held an official position in Frankfurt and in Eisenach. When Telemann refused, Duke Wilhelm Ernst's choice fell

on Drese's son who was then vice-Kapellmeister. This predictable decision must have
dealt a severe blow to Bach's self-confidence and professional pride. The post of
Kapellmeister should have been his, but the Duke had his reasons for deciding otherwise.
The appointment of the young Johann Wilhelm Drese can be seen as an expression of
professional justice, a means of showing his gratitude to the Drese family for their service
to the music at his court for three generations. It is also possible that the Duke was too
uneasy about Bach: his great ability was beyond question, as was his considerable
reputation, but he also had a tendency to insubordination. The antagonism between the
Duke and his brother was a matter of common knowledge, yet his court organist went to
play chamber music at the Red Palace and indulged his younger brother's taste for
modern Italian music. Then again, although Bach had been given a salary in excess of
that of his predecessor Effler, he had, quite soon after his appointment, auditioned at the
Liebfrauenkirche in Halle, and declined their offer only after Wilhelm Ernst had again
raised his salary and promoted him to the position of Konzertmeister. It was, perhaps,
understandable that the Duke should have regarded Bach's behaviour as unreliable,
while the proven devotion of the Drese family was reason enough to prefer them.
Therefore, Bach was not elevated from his post as Konzertmeister. This decision was to
signal the end of Bach's time in Weimar. By nature incapable of meekly accepting a
personal slight or decision that he regarded as unjust, he exhibited once again that ability
to make important decisions about his career which he had given proof of, both in
Arnstadt and Mühlhausen. He was possibly supported in his decision by Duke Johann
Ernst, through whom he had met the twenty-three-year-old Prince Leopold of Anhalt-
Cöthen; this acquaintance resulted in Bach's appointment as Hofkapellmeister of Anhalt-
Cöthen on 5 August 1717. The appointment assured the disappointed Konzertmeister of
the status he had so much desired and also entailed a further rise in his annual stipend,
which was now 400 thalers.

Bach's departure from Weimar was not, however, achieved without extreme
difficulty. He had accepted the post in Cöthen before handing in his resignation in
Weimar, and the resignation was not accepted. There was a period of stalemate, during
which Bach tried repeatedly to obtain his dismissal and the Duke, probably to punish
him for having accepted the Cöthen post, refused it. Weeks, then months passed.
Eventually Bach must have applied some kind of pressure which angered the Duke, for

*37. Dresden – the
Neumarkt (New
Market Place) with
the Church of Our
Lady.*

he was arrested on 6 November; from the Duke's point of view, this re-established his authority. On 2 December Bach was released and dismissed in disgrace. The ducal secretary wrote of this extraordinary event:

> On 6 November, the quondam Konzertmeister and Court Organist Bach was confined to the justice-room for too stubbornly forcing the issue of his dismissal, and on 2 December he was finally discharged from his post by the Court Secretary and, in disgrace, freed from detention.

Thus Bach's time at Weimar drew dramatically to a close. At the end there had been conflict, but also self-assertion on the part of the departing Konzertmeister.

The years he spent in Weimar, from 1708 to 1717, had been for Bach a period of great artistic development during which his professional experience in many different fields had increased enormously. As a composer he had now become a master: his reputation had spread far beyond the confines of Thuringia and he had established his right to be considered among the more important German musicians. His self-confidence had also increased. Shortly after obtaining his dismissal, Bach and his family made the move that had been planned for weeks.

In Cöthen, Leopold had succeeded his father in 1704, but his mother, the Duchess Gisela Agnes, had acted as regent until he attained his majority in December 1715. The Duchy of Anhalt-Cöthen had close political links with Prussia, so the young Leopold had received part of his education at the Royal Military Academy in Berlin. His sister Eleonore Wilhelmine was married in January 1716 to Prince Ernst August of Weimar.

In 1720 Cöthen (now Köthen) was a town of only about 2000 inhabitants but its social structure was affected by the fact that it was the seat of the reigning princes. Both Lutherans and members of the Reformed Church lived there in uneasy proximity. Duchess Gisela Agnes was a Lutheran, but her son was attached to the Reformed Church and apparently did not make things easy for the Lutherans. This embattled group had, at last, been allowed its own place of worship in 1699 but was still discriminated against both materially and ideologically. Among the court musicians the same religious difference

38. Memorandum of Bach's arrest and dismissal from service in Weimar.

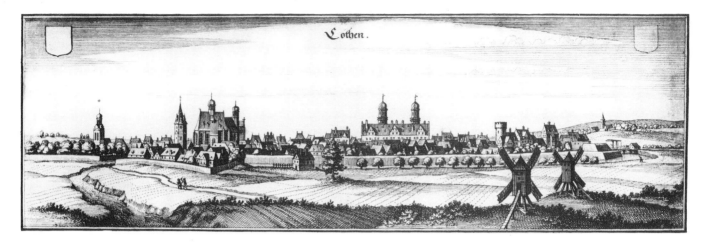

existed. The large number of complaints are sufficient to show that religious conflict, tolerated and even instigated by the Duke, was a constant hindrance to life in the small town.

The Cöthen Hofkapelle, whose primary function was to perform purely instrumental music, had only been in existence for a few years. Within a short time Leopold had enlarged it to eighteen players, and it was of this group that Bach now assumed leadership. His predecessor, Reinhard Stricker, had come from the court in Berlin in 1714, but stayed in Cöthen only until the end of July 1717, hence Bach's appointment as of 5 August. As the court of Cöthen adhered to the teachings of the Reformed Church, which meant that no elaborate music could be performed during the services, the post restricted Bach's activity in this field and only a few of his church cantatas were ever performed there. The two chief kinds of music-making were chamber music and concerts by the entire Hofkapelle, known as the *Collegium musicum.*

In later years Bach was to refer to the Duke of Cöthen as "A prince who both knew about music and loved it". Leopold had received most of his musical education from Johann David Heinichen (later to become an influential Hofkapellmeister in Dresden); he played an active part in the music at his court, being particularly proficient on the viola da gamba, capable of playing the violin and harpsichord, and reportedly possessing a good bass voice as well. The Duke's musicianship certainly made for very good relations with his Kapellmeister from the beginning and had been doubtless one reason for his engaging Bach as quickly as he had.

Among the officials and attendants at the court of Cöthen, the position of Hofkapellmeister ranked on a par with that of the chamberlain and was therefore a high one. The salary was in keeping with the proportion of the ducal budget that was allocated to court music (not less than three per cent of the total). Of Bach's actual salary nothing is now known as the records have not survived, but the extent of his duties can be inferred from documents relating to the local situation and comparable conditions at other courts. He was responsible for all the music at court. Vocal soloists were engaged now and then, but he had no choir, there was no opera, and only, as we have already said, minimal church music. Music was primarily used as an adjunct to social life: it was for entertainment, for enhancing the pomp of ceremonial occasions, celebrations of birthdays, or the visits of important guests. Presumably the more intimate kinds of music-making were those in which the court indulged most frequently, for it was in these that the music-loving Duke could himself take part.

The rehearsals of the Hofkapelle took place every week in a room in Bach's house, and for this he received, as his predecessor had done, an annual contribution towards his rent. The rooms in which Bach lived during his time in Cöthen have unfortunately disappeared. There was no organ at his disposal to compare with the one in Weimar, and though there was a small instrument in the palace chapel, it was not part of his duties to play it. This did not mean, however, that he broke off all his links with the organ. He was probably still in Weimar when he received the invitation that resulted in his travelling to Leipzig on 16 December 1717 (only a few days after his arrival in Cöthen) to test the

Paulinerkirche organ, which had recently been repaired and enlarged. His report, dated 17 December, is signed "Johann Sebastian Bach, Kapellmeister to his Highness the Prince of Anhalt-Cöthen, etc." It was indeed a strange stroke of fate that took him, on his first trip away from Cöthen, to the place where he was eventually to live for twenty-seven years.

Although the Duke already had some notion of Bach's ability from the time of their meeting in Weimar, his new Kapellmeister would have been at pains to impress his employer. We may safely assume that he lost no time in getting to know the musicians he was working with and in assessing their capabilities. One of his duties was to produce a new composition for any occasion as required, but apart from cantatas of homage written for special occasions such as birthdays, we have no precise information about which works were performed on which occasions.

Certainly many of Bach's compositions, some written in earlier years, were in the Cöthen repertoire alongside the works of other composers. There was, however, only a small collection of music available, and during his time in Cöthen Bach enlarged it considerably. It was one of Bach's enduring traits that wherever he went he would collect, study and perform as much of the music of other composers as he possibly could. The nature of his work in Cöthen also meant that he had to make additions to the instruments at his disposal; thus we find him travelling to Berlin, probably at the beginning of March 1719, to purchase the "large, two-manual harpsichord" which had been ordered from the builder Michael Mietke and to arrange for its shipment to Cöthen. It was on this trip that Bach performed before the Margrave Christian Ludwig of Brandenburg in the Berlin Palace, who was so impressed that he immediately commissioned Bach to write several pieces for him. Concerts were occasionally given in Cöthen on festive and state occasions for which the regular musicians were not sufficient and extra performers had to be summoned from such places as Rudolstadt, Merseburg, Halle and Leipzig.

Early in the summer of 1719 Bach heard that George Frideric Handel was visiting his mother in neighbouring Halle, the town of his birth. Anxious to make the acquaintance of the celebrated musician, Bach travelled to Halle, only to find, so reports tell us, that the visitor had already left. Another attempt to meet Handel, this time while Bach was working in Leipzig, was to be equally unsuccessful. On both occasions the initiative was taken by Bach, which is hardly surprising considering that Handel was a musician of considerably greater world renown.

On 15 November 1719 Maria Barbara gave birth to a son, Leopold Augustus, who was to be her last child. On the baptismal register of the Cöthen court chapel, the list of godparents is headed by the name of the ruling Prince, Leopold, followed by that of his brother Augustus Ludwig and then their sister, the Duchess Eleonore Wilhelmine. This is an indication of the extraordinarily good relations that must have existed between Bach and the ducal family. The baby Leopold Augustus died at the age of only ten months, his burial being entered in the register of the Agnuskirche on 28 September 1719.

During his first years in Cöthen, Bach twice accompanied the Duke on trips to Carlsbad, then a famous spa and a meeting-place for the rich ruling families, where it was a matter of prestige that Leopold should appear with a section of his court orchestra. For

41. Karlsbad – panoramic view.

Bach, these trips were not only a welcome break from his usual round of duties in Cöthen, but they also provided him with an excellent opportunity to meet other musicians and hear new music. It was on his return from the second of these trips that Bach learnt of the sudden death of his wife. The register gives the date of her burial as 7 July 1720. The *Nekrolog* describes the occurrence thus:

> After 13 years of happy marriage with his first wife, he was met with grievous sorrow in the year 1720 when, upon his return to Cöthen from a journey to Carlsbad with his Prince, he found her dead and buried although he had left her hale and hearty upon his departure. The first news of her falling ill and then dying was given him as he entered his house.

The very cornerstone of Bach's family life had crumbled. His four children, Catharina Dorothea, Wilhelm Friedemann, Carl Philipp Emanuel and Gottfried Bernhard had lost their mother, and Bach, heavily occupied with the professional demands being made on him day in and day out by his position as Kapellmeister, had also now to assume the household responsibilities which before had fallen to his wife. On top of this, the sense of personal loss must have been very great indeed; so great, in fact, that it is possible that he had serious thoughts of giving up his post in Cöthen as a direct result of it. Whether or not this was a factor, he certainly undertook a journey to Hamburg in the autumn to offer himself as a candidate for the vacant post of organist at the Jakobikirche. During this stay he played on the organ of the Katharinenkirche in the presence of the elderly Reinken whose playing had so impressed him as a young man. This time it was the turn of Reinken to be impressed. The *Nekrolog* describes the occasion in some detail:

> At this time, probably in 1722, he travelled to Hamburg and played for two hours before the municipal council and many other prominent citizens of the town on the fine organ of the Catharinenkirche, causing general astonishment. The aged organist of this church, Johann Adam Reinken, then almost one hundred years old, listened with especial pleasure, particularly to his rendering of the chorale *By the waters of Babylon* upon which our Bach, in response to a request from those present, improvised for almost half an hour most extensively and in the most varied way, as used to be the custom of the best Hamburg organists at the Saturday vespers, whereupon he paid him the following compliment: "I thought that this art was dead, but I see that it still lives on in you." This pronouncement by Reinken was all the more unexpected in that, many years before, he had himself elaborated upon this very chorale in the manner described above. Bach was not unaware of this, nor of the fact that he had always been of a somewhat envious disposition. Reinken called our Bach up to him and showed him much courtesy.

Bach was unable to take part in the actual audition as he had to return to Cöthen to prepare the music for Duke Leopold's birthday celebrations, and on 23 November he went home. Had he succeeded at the audition, it might have proved an expensive victory, for it was still the custom in Hamburg for an organist to buy his appointment. The pastor at the Jakobikirche at this time was Erdmann Neumeister, whose importance in the development of the text for church cantatas has already been noted.

During 1721 the idea of marrying again became more and more attractive to Bach. Some time before the autumn of 1720, at a concert in Cöthen, he had met the twenty-year-old Anna Magdalena Wilcke, a soprano of outstanding quality who was attached to the neighbouring court of Zerbst. She was the youngest daughter of Johann Caspar Wilcke, a trumpeter at the Weissenfels court who had previously been employed in Zeitz.

Attraction and mutual esteem must have blossomed quickly for Bach and Anna Magdalena were married on 3 December 1721. The entry in the register of the court chapel reads:

> On 3 December Herr Johann Sebastian Bach, Capell-Meister to His Highness the Prince, and widower, And Jungfer [Miss] Anna Magdalena, spinster, legitimate daughter of Herr Johann Caspar Wülckeln, court and field trumpeter to His Highness the Prince of Saxe-Weissenfels, were married at home by command of the Prince.

Just one week later, however, a wedding of much greater splendour took place when Duke Leopold married Princess Friederica Henrietta of Anhalt-Bernburg. Bach was later to describe the Princess (in a letter to his friend Erdmann written in 1730) as an "amusa" — a woman entirely devoid of any artistic sensibility — and to hold her responsible for the decline in Leopold's musical inclinations.

The year 1720–21 marked a turning-point in Bach's fortunes at Cöthen. The earlier years, when he had built up the orchestra, had been a time of progress and affirmation. Now Maria Barbara's death, his unresolved application to Hamburg, and a steady diminution of his orchestral forces all combined to make him see Cöthen in a less rosy light. Why the Duke should have decided to reduce expenditure on his court music is unclear, but for Bach this meant a reduction in his own field of activity which, although the measures were not aimed at him specifically, cannot have left him unaffected.

Neither Bach's patently happy second marriage nor anything else that happened could halt or reverse a process which Bach felt was frustrating him both mentally and in his profession. And his innate tendency to examine his current circumstances and make a critical assessment of his potentialities was once again manifest.

An outline of the works that Bach composed in Cöthen will give some idea of the emphases dictated by professional demands and of the direction his musical interests took in these years, though it should be borne in mind that our knowledge is nowhere near complete. A considerable number of his compositions from this period have been lost, and although some of the material was re-worked in Leipzig, during his time there, much has disappeared irretrievably.

It would have been impossible for Bach to have fulfilled his duties as Court Kapellmeister without producing a succession of orchestral suites, concertos for various combinations of instruments, overtures and chamber music in quantities much greater than

43

have survived. And there is no doubt now that, of the few overtures, concertos and sonatas previously ascribed to the Cöthen period, some at least belong to the years in Leipzig. However, the "six concertos for various instruments" now known as the Brandenburg Concertos (BWV 1046–1051) were certainly written in Cöthen. These were the works composed in response to the commission of the Margrave Christian Ludwig of Brandenburg in 1719; Bach had them bound in one volume and added a long dedication. These marvellous pieces, possessed of an individuality and originality unequalled by any other comparable works of their time, are the result of Bach's increased experience with the concerto. And he may have written many other similar works which have now been lost. In addition to orchestral works with concertino, Bach also wrote concertos for one solo instrument while he was in Cöthen. The violin concertos were, until recently, assumed to have been written around 1720; the date has now been questioned, but this type of violin concerto is certainly of the sort that would have been required of him in Cöthen. One such example is the A minor Concerto for violin and string orchestra (BWV 1041) which, like the other concertos, was later adapted as a harpsichord concerto in Leipzig.

The six suites and partitas for solo violin without basso continuo are also dated 1720, and the six suites for cello (BWV 1007–1012) also belong apparently to the same period; they are assumed to have been written for Ferdinand Christian Abel, the outstanding player of the viola da gamba and cello in the Cöthen court orchestra. These two sets are of a quality far above anything else that had been written for unaccompanied string instruments at that time. Since chamber music was undoubtedly of such great importance in Cöthen, it seems logical to attribute the majority of Bach's sonatas for one or two solo instruments and continuo to the years around 1720. These works occupy a place of especial importance in musical history in that they raise the status of the harpsichord from that of a continuo member to that of an independent solo instrument. At Cöthen Bach wrote several collections of keyboard music. The first of these was the *Wilhelm Friedemann Bach Notebook*, which carries the date 22 January 1720 on its title-page — the date on which composition of it began. It was followed in 1722 by the first of the *Notebooks For Anna Magdalena Bach* (for which no more precise date is available). This was probably only started in Cöthen and later finished in Leipzig. These collections, to which the dedicatees themselves contributed,[6] are both documents of the keyboard playing that took place in the home, and also allow us to see Bach as the teacher. The date 1722 is also to be found at the bottom of the title page of the collection which Bach called *The Well Tempered Clavier*, the famous series of twenty-four preludes and fugues which rely on a system of equal temperament in the tuning of the instrument by which all the keys of the chromatic scale, major and minor, become available. This was a landmark in the history of keyboard playing and composition. In 1744 Bach wrote a second book of *The Well Tempered Clavier* in Leipzig, but the designation, First and Second Parts, is incorrect, since it suggests that the First Part was incomplete, which is not the case. Towards the end of his time in Cöthen, Bach wrote another collection of keyboard works: *The Inventions and Sinfonias*. The title page is dated 1723, and Bach still signs himself "Kapellmeister of Anhalt-Cöthen".

Among the works which were definitely written in Cöthen are the birthday cantata for "Most Illustrious Leopold" (BWV 173a) and the New Year cantata, *Die Zeit, die Tag' und Jahre macht* ("Time, of which the days and years are made") BWV 134a. Both contain material that Bach later re-worked for sacred music.

Even an incomplete survey such as this indicates that Bach's creative development was being influenced less by chance than by method. It shows, at all events, a high degree of deliberation that allowed Bach to fulfil simultaneously the demands of his post and his own artistic interests and fuse them in a highly individual way. This attitude was to become still more strongly marked in his later years, so that we see his work, not as so

many examples of different *genres*, but as a grand total, the parts of which are "fragments of a great confession" in an almost Goethean way. His compositions are never "court music" in the narrow sense, but reach far beyond such conventional limitations, combining the craftsmanship of a master with a highly individual imagination and a remarkably modern dynamic quality.

His personality was compounded of strong convictions, consistency, a highly developed sense of his responsibilities to his art, to his family and to life itself, all welded into one. If we try to imagine what Bach actually looked like in his mid-thirties, we must assume that the features were already marked by the tribulations of life. He had had to come to terms with death, too. Within his own family he had lost his first wife, three of his children, one brother, Johann Christoph, in Ohrdruf, and another, Johann Jakob, in Stockholm.

On 5 June 1722 Johann Kuhnau, the greatly respected Cantor at the Leipzig Thomasschule, died. He had been more than an able cantor, making important contributions to the development of his art while upholding its traditions. Leipzig was a town that pulsated with life. It was a commercial town of busy markets and flourishing trade, the arts and sciences were well developed and forward-looking, and it had long attached great importance to music. The appointment of a new cantor for the Thomasschule proved to be a difficult task for the town council in the months following Kuhnau's death. Initially, Telemann offered himself as a candidate, but after being informed of his acceptance he withdrew the application to remain, with an improvement to his position, in Hamburg. Of the other candidates who had applied, the council was giving serious consideration to Christoph Graupner, the distinguished Kapellmeister at the court of Darmstadt. His prince, however, refused to release him and he informed Bach about the vacancy. Meanwhile, Johann Friedrich Fasch, court Kapellmeister in Zerbst, had refused the post on hearing that he was also expected to teach Latin. All these difficulties over the choice of a new cantor for the Thomasschule were common knowledge among the musical fraternity, and it was natural that Bach should also learn about them. In December 1722 he applied for the post and on 7 February auditioned at the Thomaskirche with a performance of his cantata *Jesus nahm zu sich die Zwölve* ("Jesus took the twelve unto Him" BWV 22). The fact that he auditioned for the post by no means implies that he had already made up his mind that he wanted to go to Leipzig. There were a great many factors to be considered first, both for and against the move: in Cöthen he was respected and appreciated, but his working conditions were deteriorating; he was well paid, but prospects for the education of his sons were not as good in Cöthen as they would be in Leipzig with its university and rich musical tradition. And he now had the chance of a respected post there. He took it. In the first half of April Bach handed in his resignation to Prince Leopold, thus preparing the way for an offer from the Leipzig town council. At Easter, Bach was again in Leipzig and on 19 April he wrote to the Council to inform its members of his provisional acceptance of the cantorship at the Thomasschule indicating that he would accept their nomination and the conditions of the office.

> Whereas I, the undersigned, have presented to the most worthy Council of Leipzig my candidacy for the vacant post of Cantor to the Thomas-Schule in that place, and have respectfully requested that I be considered in this connection, now therefore I hereby pledge myself that if my request be granted and the said post be entrusted to me, I will not only within three or, at the most, four weeks from this date make myself free of the engagement given me at the court of the Prince of Anhalt-Cöthen, and convey to the said Council the certificate of dismissal I receive, but also, if I should enter upon the duties of the said post of Cantor, conduct myself according to the School regulations now in effect or to be put into effect; and especially I will instruct the boys admitted to the School not only in the regular classes established for that purpose, but also, without special compensation, in private singing lessons. I

will also faithfully attend to whatever else is incumbent upon me, and furthermore, but not without the previous knowledge and consent of a most worthy Council, in case someone should be needed to assist me in the instruction of the Latin language, will faithfully and without ado compensate the said person out of my own pocket, without desiring anything from the most worthy Council or otherwise. In witness whereof I have executed this pledge under my hand and seal. Written in Leipzig on 19 April 1723. Johann Sebastian Bach: Capellmeister to the Prince of Anhalt-Cöthen.

The way was now clear. On 22 April the Town Council elected Bach to the Cantorship of St Thomas's. Bach accepted. On 5 May he signed the final undertaking, and three days later was examined by the Professor of Theology Johann Schmid and the Superintendent Salomon Deyling; then he was sworn in and his appointment was finally confirmed by the Consistory. On 15 May he received his first salary, and his time as a Hofkapellmeister was over. He had spent no less than fifteen years in the service of the courts, first of Weimar and then of Cöthen, and now stood at the pinnacle of German musical life. Naturally, in the years that followed, he never lost touch with the music of the courts — he even renewed his connections — but in his post in Leipzig, which he was to hold until his death, he returned to the kind of music with which he had begun in Arnstadt and Mühlhausen; but it was a return at the very highest level.

45. *Leipzig – St Thomas's Church, seen from the east.*

Cantor at the Thomasschule and Director of Music in Leipzig

Last Saturday at noon, four wagons arrived here from Cöthen laden with the household effects belonging to the former Kapellmeister at the court of the Prince of that place who has now been invited to become Cantor in Leipzig. At two o'clock he himself arrived with his family in two coaches and moved into the newly-renovated residence at the Thomasschule.

Thus were the readers of a newspaper informed about the Bach family's move to Leipzig. Johann Sebastian himself was already somewhat familiar with the town; he had been there on several occasions including the time in 1717 when he tested the organ in the Paulinerkirche. Even so, for the entire family Leipzig was a new world, with its exciting big-town atmosphere, its bewildering array of streets, alleys, and squares, its impressive buildings and its throngs of people, residents and visitors, rich and poor, nobles, merchants and craftsmen. The population of Leipzig numbered about 35,000 at that time. An analysis of the town's social structure reveals that the vast majority of the inhabitants belonged to the bourgeois and working classes. Available in Leipzig were workers and self-employed members of craftsmen's guilds, small shopkeepers, functionaries, influential traders and merchants, and members of the nobility who also held a job. Men of science, teachers, and artists (including professional musicians) made up only a small proportion of the population. The welfare of the town largely depended upon its trade, and Leipzig trade fairs were part of a tradition which had existed for hundreds of years.

Large trading houses with central courtyards, through-passages and workshops, built on a palatial scale that proclaimed their owners' wealth and influence, were a feature of the town. By the time that the Bach family moved to Leipzig, over a third of all the houses were five storeys tall, and those belonging to the rich men in power were manifestly imposing. Only fifteen years after Bach's death, Johann Wolfgang von Goethe, then a student, was deeply impressed by a Leipzig which still retained the same characteristics. He wrote:

> Leipzig does not put the observer in mind of times long past, but rather does he read in these monuments the signs of a recent epoch, an epoch of trade, prosperity and wealth. The buildings were very much to my taste with their vast size — as it seemed to me then — and their high façades fronting on to two streets and enclosing, in their courtyards, a whole world of bourgeois trade and culture as if they had been great castles or even small towns in themselves.

The town was the economic centre of the state of Saxony. It had no resident ruler and had even absolved itself of any obligation to provide for the Elector of Saxony and his retinue when he visited Leipzig. As a centre of early bourgeois life in Germany, only Hamburg could rival Leipzig. A town of great architectural beauty, it also boasted many well-planned and expensively laid-out parks and gardens. Underground sewers, streets paved for the sake of hygiene and elegance, the presence of street lighting and the suppression of its fort-like characteristics, had given the town a thoroughly modern "feel". This corresponded with a certain open-mindedness in cultural and scientific matters and considerable self-confidence. Naturally, the people of Leipzig did not all think alike. The convictions, both religious and otherwise, even within the middle classes, differed according to conflations of tradition or the newer, more unconventional attitudes. Contradictions were to be found within theological and ecclesiastical circles, in the schools, in the council, among the townspeople and also in the town's relations with the court at Dresden. Learned societies of various kinds, like the Society for Contemporary German Poetry which was founded in 1723, were established and these, with their encyclopedic orientation, had a vast influence on the printing trade. Leipzig acted as a centre not only for the distribution of goods, but also of literature. There were ideological clashes at the university, for instance, where, among the theologians and the students of law, the orthodox and idealistic elements were constantly at loggerheads with the rationalists imbued with the ideas of the early Enlightenment about such matters as tolerance and universality. Divisions between the groups were not always clear; often views which seemed to their supporters to be diametrically opposed, in reality shared much common ground. The most important theological conflict, in Leipzig as elsewhere, was that between Orthodoxy and Pietism. Here it was the orthodox Lutheran view that prevailed, though it must be said that theological dissension was by no means a major preoccupation of the general public, to whom the sciences and the search for practical knowledge of use to trade and industry were of much greater value than theological argument.

The arts — poetry, music, painting, and drama — were also much in demand.

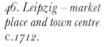

46. Leipzig – market place and town centre c.1712.

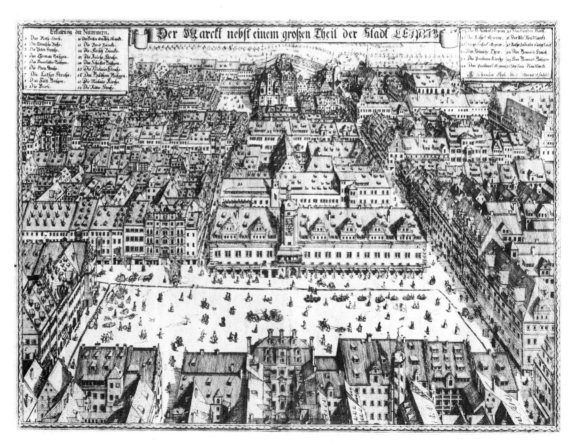

Io. Chunau. Musicus. —

Johannes Henricus Ernesti
Post Prof Publicus Academia Decem ir
Scholæ Thomanæ Rector.

During Bach's time in Leipzig, the most influential figure on the literary scene was
Johann Christoph Gottsched, an exponent of the early period of the Enlightenment in
German Literature, who was motivated by both rationalism and nationalism. That he
was anxious to combine theory and practice is borne out by his collaboration with
Caroline Neuber, the dominant figure in the German theatre of the time who gave over
700 performances in Leipzig.

Musical life in Leipzig had been varied and colourful for a long time. Its characteristics were determined by the Church, by secular ceremonial, the theatre, private and
public entertainment, and the beginnings of the bourgeois habit of concert-going. From
1693 until 1720 the town had boasted an opera house, and was one of the few places
where early German opera was cultivated. This art form had, however, created problems
as far as church music was concerned, for, as Bach's predecessor, Kuhnau, had explained
to the town council, the best singers and instrumentalists had deserted him in favour of
the lure of the opera. This was to be one of Bach's problems too.

Bach's final undertaking, which he signed on 5 May, sets out and confirms all the
most important functions and duties that were expected of the Cantor at the Thomasschule:

1) That I shall set the boys a shining example of an honest, retiring manner of
   life, serve the school industriously, and instruct the boys conscientiously;
2) Bring the music in both the principal Churches of this town into good repute, to
   the best of my ability;
3) Show to Their Excellencies the Councillors all proper respect and obedience,
   and protect and further everywhere as best I may their honour and reputation,
   likewise if a gentleman of the Council requires the boys for a musical occasion to
   provide him unhesitatingly with the same but otherwise never permit them to
   leave the town to attend funerals or weddings without the previous knowledge
   and consent of the Mayor and the current Board of School Directors;
4) Give due obedience to Their Excellencies the Inspectors and Directors of the
   school and follow every instruction they may issue in the name of the Council;

49. Leipzig – the council chamber of the old town hall where Bach signed his acknowledgement as Thomascantor on 5.5.1723.

5) Not to accept any boys into the school who do not already have a good grounding in music, or who are not at least suitable to receive such instruction, nor to do the same without the prior knowledge and consent of the Inspectors and Board of Directors;

6) In order to avoid unnecessary expense on the part of the Churches, to faithfully instruct the boys not only in vocal music but also in instrumental music;

7) With the object of maintaining good order in the Churches, to so arrange the music that it does not last too long, and shall be of a kind that does not make an operatic impression but rather incite the listeners to devotion;

8) Provide the new Church with good pupils;

9) Treat the boys in a friendly and gentle manner, but in cases of disobedience to use a moderate amount of chastisement or report them to the proper place;

10) Attend faithfully to the instruction in the school and to whatever else it is fitting for me to do;

11) And if I cannot undertake this myself, arrange that it be done by some other capable person without expense to Their Excellencies the Councillors or to the School;

12) Not to leave the town without the permission of the current Mayor;

13) Whenever possible to walk always with the boys at funerals, as is customary;

14) And not accept or wish to accept any office in the University without the consent of the honourable members of the Council.

I hereby undertake and bind myself to observe faithfully all of the above requirements, and on pain of losing my post not to act contrary to them. In witness whereof I have set my hand and seal to this agreement. Executed in Leipzig, 5 May 1723. Johann Sebastian Bach.

This document was intended as a guide to conduct. It also contained stipulations, as Bach must have realized, that were to cause him inconvenience on many occasions. Because both the school and choir of St Thomas's had been part of the municipality since the Reformation, Bach was a servant of the town. As Cantor, he was of course simultaneously responsible to his superintendent and the consistory where church music was concerned. The interests of the two parties naturally clashed at times, and there was a certain amount of wrangling over responsibilities as a matter of course; the consequences of such disputes were felt nowhere more strongly than in the cantorship, because the incumbent was dependent upon both the town and the church. As Cantor at the Thomasschule Bach was also Director of Music for the town of Leipzig. The town musicians were responsible to him and their co-operation was indispensable. However, Bach had no authority in the university. Contrary to tradition, the university did not appoint the new Cantor (who was not an academic) as their Director of Music, and this was to remain a bone of contention for a long time.

For the Bach family, life in a large town was something that they could only come to terms with gradually. The Cantor's lodging was in the south wing of the Thomasschule, facing the gate. It occupied the first three storeys and was flanked on the ground floor by the school refectory, on the first by classrooms, and on the second by rehearsal rooms and meeting room. The north wing, facing the church, housed the Rector's lodging. The church and its surrounding cluster of dwellings formed an independent architectural entity beside the churchyard, which was not far from the central market-place dominated by its impressive Renaissance town-hall. Passing through St Thomas's Gate, one reached an open area to the west of the town consisting of gardens and meadows, over which, from all the west windows of their home, the Bachs had a beautiful view. The church itself was at the centre of the cluster of buildings and divided them into northern and

50. The surroundings of Leipzig – view to the west, approximately as Bach would have seen from his home.

51. Leipzig – St Thomas's Church before renovation in 1885.

southern wings each with a cobbled courtyard. The southern courtyard, as if to emphasize its more secular role, boasted a stone fountain, and it was around this courtyard that the Bach's family life revolved.

52. Leipzig – St Thomas's church-yard with the extended Thomasschule on the left beside the church.

The thirty-eight-year-old Cantor and his twenty-two-year-old wife already had five children when they moved into their new quarters at the Thomasschule. Four of the children were from Bach's first marriage. Catharina Dorothea was now fifteen, Wilhelm Friedemann thirteen, Carl Philipp Emanuel nine and Gottfried Bernhard eight. Christiana Sophia Henrietta was only three months old. Wilhelm Friedemann and Carl Philipp Emanuel entered the Thomasschule as day-boys on 14 June 1723, followed later by Gottfried Bernhard.

When he assumed the post at St Thomas's, Bach's professional life underwent a radical change. In Arnstadt and Mühlhausen his work had been relatively simple; in Cöthen he had gained experience with a competent orchestra but had no choir at his disposal; in Weimar, as in Cöthen, he had been in the service of a court, but had been denied the coveted status of Kapellmeister; now, in Leipzig, he had at last a situation which allowed him to exploit his varied experience and his artistic skills to the full, for here he was Cantor, Kapellmeister, and Director of Municipal Music all at one and the same time. In Leipzig he arrived at a new stage of his life.

Naturally Bach did not relinquish the comfortable salary he already enjoyed in Cöthen without a careful consideration of the financial prospects of his new position. His income at Leipzig was derived from a variety of sources, a much larger proportion than before coming from earnings outside his salary. The basic salary paid by the Council to the Cantor was modest, but over and above it he received money for wood and light, sixteen bushels of corn, two cords of split logs, and two jugs of wine at Easter, Whitsun and Christmas. Additional income also came regularly from endowments. These were sums that had been bequeathed for memorial performances of songs and chorales. Lastly, the Cantor also received payment for the St Thomas choir's participation at weddings and funerals and a portion from the collections taken during choral processions. In a letter that he wrote on 28 October 1730 to Georg Erdmann, Bach estimated his total annual income in Leipzig to be around 700 thalers. This was a considerable improvement over his earnings at Cöthen. In the same letter he complained, however, about the high cost of living in Leipzig, and admitted that the total fluctuated according to the additions to his salary that he was able to earn:

> My present post brings me in about 700 thalers, and when there are rather more deaths than usual my incidental income rises accordingly; but when the air is healthy it falls like it did last year, when I earned over 100 thalers less in "incidentals" than usual. But in Thuringia I could do more with 400 thalers than I can here with the same sum because of the excessively costly way of life.

*53. St Matthew
Passion, BWV 244 –
first page of the
autograph score.*

Professionally, Bach's main responsibility was to the cantorship. He had to ensure the provision of music in the principal churches, among which St Thomas and St Nicholas were the most important artistically. This entailed working daily with the choir, organizing the instrumentalists, and, besides, looking after all the musical material. Bach extricated himself from the duty of teaching Latin by appointing a deputy teacher at his own expense. He was clearly determined to make the performances of cantatas on Sundays and feast-days the focus of his musical activity. It was on these occasions that he was able to combine his vocal and instrumental resources; it was then that he could demonstrate, through his own compositions, his skills and his knowledge and bring a real influence to bear upon the musical life of Leipzig. Using the experience that he had gained in Weimar as his starting-point, Bach produced, from the summer of 1723 until the end of the decade, a wonderful series of cantatas. Nearly sixty of these were required annually for the services on Sundays and feast-days, their texts usually linked to the Gospel for the day. The performances alternated between St Nicholas's and St Thomas's, the former having priority because it was where the superintendent, Samuel Deyling, who was the cantor's superior, was in charge. In the order of service, the cantata came before the sermon, and was not supposed to last longer than thirty minutes as time was needed afterwards for the Communion. If the cantata was in two parts, the sermon was given between them. Toward the beginning of his time in Leipzig, Bach jotted down the order of service for the first Sunday in Advent on the back of the title page of a cantata:

(1) Prelude. (2) Motet. (3) Prelude based on the theme of the Kyrie, music only. (4) Intoning before the altar. (5) Reading of the Epistle. (6) Sung Litany. (7) Prelude on the theme of the Chorale. (8) Reading of the Gospel. (9) Prelude to the main music. (10) Sung Creed. (11) The sermon. (12) After the sermon, the usual singing of a few verses of a hymn. (13) *Verba Institutionis.* (14) Prelude on the music. And after this, Prelude and Chorale sung alternately, etc.

When one considers that Bach had to compose a cantata virtually every week, year in, year out, that he had to supervise at least the preparation of the musical parts, had to direct the performances and still fulfil many additional duties, one begins to have some idea of the workload carried by this diligent and hard-working cantor.

Although the cantatas, which used both voices and instruments, formed the core of Bach's church music, he turned more than once to the larger-scale form of the oratorio, for his Passions. These were designed for performances on Good Friday. He wrote the St John Passion in 1723, at the beginning of his time in Leipzig when he was working on church music with an extraordinary intensity. The St Matthew Passion came, however, towards the end of this period, in 1727–29. Setting the story of Christ's Passion to music belongs to a very old and very complex tradition which reached its full flowering in these works by Bach. The first version of the St John Passion was performed at the church of St Nicholas on Good Friday, 1724. The second version was first heard on Good Friday (30 March) in 1725. It used to be thought that the first performance of the St Matthew Passion was on Good Friday, 1729, but it may well have been completed two years earlier and first given in 1727 (11 April). Quite apart from the unique quality of Bach's Passions, it must be realized that these musical masterpieces are very closely bound to the theological and scriptural content of the service. Preparations for the performance of these works put a great strain on Bach and also caused a measure of friction in his life. When, in the middle of March 1739, the Council forbade him to perform a Passion and Bach replied resignedly that it would, in any case, be "just a burden", we can detect a distinct note of bitterness in his words.

Tension had been building up between Bach and his superiors, both secular and

ecclesiastical, since the end of the 1720s. Neither side was solely to blame. Bach treated his profession and his work with a seriousness that was part of his character, and he believed in maintaining an equitable balance between his rights and his duties. He could not and would not accept that his authority as Cantor should be any less than that accorded to his predecessor, and objected strongly when any disputes over his authority were settled to his disadvantage, by which he also meant, the disadvantage of his position. Problems of this kind were unavoidable. Between 1723 and 1726 he was in dispute with the university over the tradition by which the Thomascantor and the Director of Music at the university should be held by the same man. He failed. In 1728 he sought the support of the Town Council against a decision of the consistory which reassigned the Cantor's right to choose the hymns for the service to the deacon (thus favouring the priest over the Cantor).

As far as the actual content of the document is concerned, the most important of Bach's petitions to the Council was the one he wrote on 23 August 1730 entitled "Short but most necessary outline for a well-appointed church music; with certain modest reflec-

54. Heading of the petition of 23.8.1730 to the Leipzig City Council, autograph.

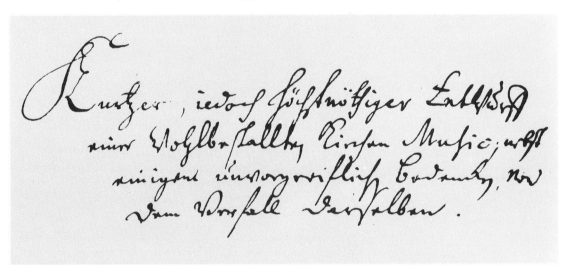

tions on the decline of the same".[7] In this memorandum Bach sought to inform the council about the essential requirements for the cultivation of music in the church. He analysed the situation in Leipzig, referred to the change in musical taste and recommended the general direction in which Leipzig's church music should be developed with the assistance of the Town Council. Bach's Outline may also be the way he chose to reply to the very severe criticism of the Cantor that had been made in a session of the council on 2 August 1730. The minutes include mention of Bach's negligence and stubbornness, possible referring to contraventions of the undertaking he had made at the time of his appointment. Bach, however, was not invited to be present at the session and was therefore unable to defend himself. Two days after the date of the Short Outline, Mayor Born reported a conversation he had had with Bach in the interim, in which the latter reportedly showed himself to have "little desire to work". Bach's memorandum is not mentioned, possibly because it had not yet been submitted. The council decided to reduce the Cantor's pay and the decision was implemented four weeks later when the extra emoluments were distributed. Bach received nothing at all — the evidence of ill-will is strong indeed.

The Cantor's relationship with the rector of the Thomasschule, his immediate superior, was of the utmost significance. Until 1729 the principal of the school was Johann Heinrich Ernesti, himself a former pupil of St Thomas's. Bach's relationship with him was businesslike and amiable. He was succeeded in 1730 by Johann Matthias Gesner, whom Bach had known in Weimar and whose attitude towards the Cantor was one of understanding and respect. When he left in 1734, however, the real problems began. The new headmaster was Johann August Ernesti, a man twenty-two years younger than Bach who was determined to improve the general standard of education in the school at the expense of musical training. There was no way in which the ambitious young principal and the Cantor could ever see eye to eye. Tension and discord were inevitable, and for Bach, who was dependent upon Ernesti, life must have been very difficult indeed. So here were two men, both with similar values which could have made them allies, involved in a continual antagonistic confrontation because they were unable to discover any grounds for compromise.

The tension between the two was brought to the point of open conflict over the affair of the school prefects. The prefect was supposed to assist the Cantor, but the headmaster took it upon himself to select a boy of whom Bach disapproved. That the headmaster had bypassed him in making the choice was the basis of an argument that was to last for years and that gave rise to a number of petitions. The insinuations made and the measures taken add up to a depressing picture of two men fighting for supremacy. So many and various were the problems that weighed upon Bach from the end of the 1720s that he had serious thoughts about leaving Leipzig altogether. In October 1730 he wrote to his friend Georg Erdmann:

> First of all, I find that the employment here is not nearly as lucrative as I was led to believe; secondly, many of the emoluments of the post have ceased to exist; thirdly, this is a very expensive place; and, fourthly, the authorities are odd and little devoted to music, so I am almost constantly vexed, envied and persecuted and shall soon find it necessary, with God's help, to seek my fortune elsewhere.

This was not the first time that Bach had found himself in a strife-ridden situation. No period of his life had been entirely free from conflict, and he was not of a disposition to shun a battle when he felt it was necessary to fight. Nevertheless, these years were filled with many other activities.

There were plenty of opportunities for orchestral work. A small orchestra was needed to perform the music in church on Sundays and feast-days, and because the musicians supplied by the town were by no means sufficient, Bach, like other Cantors before him, drew on the students at the university. This orchestra performed at the churches of St Thomas, St Nicholas, the New Church and, of course, at St Paul's, the university church. In the spring of 1729 Bach also became the director of the Collegium Musicum. Founded by Georg Philipp Telemann in 1702, it had been directed since 1720 by Georg Balthasar Schott, the organist at the New Church. Bach had been associated with this orchestra for many years when Schott left to become Cantor at Gotha, and the succession devolved naturally upon him. In a letter written on 20 March 1729, we find the following post-script: "The latest news is that our dear God has provided for the esteemed Herr Schott, presenting him with the Gotha cantorship, this coming week he will bid us farewell and I shall be in charge of his Collegium."

The Collegium Musicum was the mainstay of secular music in Leipzig; when Bach assumed its direction, he had occasion to utilize the experience he had already gained at the courts of Cöthen and Weimar. The orchestra met regularly for rehearsal and gave the people of Leipzig a weekly opportunity to take part in public music-making, which was then in its infancy. From these occasions the *Grosses Konzert* and the *Gewandhaus Konzert* were to develop in 1743 and 1781 respectively. Bach directed this orchestra from 1729 until 1737 and then again from 1739 until at least 1741. Various notices dating from these years announce the performances which in summer were given on Wednesday evenings from six to eight in Gottfried Zimmermann's coffee-garden and in winter on Friday evenings from eight to ten in Zimmermann's coffee-house.

Whether or not Bach consciously saw his work with the Collegium as a way of

55. Leipzig – interior of the New Church.

safeguarding his control over the instrumentalists he needed for the church, or whether his interest in his cantorial duties had diminished under the pressure of unresolved problems and conflicts, the transformation of the orchestra from "Schott's band" into "Bach's band" stimulated his musicianship. As his attention was diverted from the cantorship his commitment to cantata composition, so strong from 1723 until 1728, gradually weakened. There is no doubt at all that this work with the Collegium, which gave Bach the opportunity to perform before a wider public, became of even greater importance as the difficulties he encountered as Cantor became ever more onerous.

Bach's problems in Leipzig were typical of those faced by professional musicians in Germany in the early eighteenth century. Whether one worked for the town or the church, professional life was riddled with limitations imposed by local traditions in various stages of evolution, and personalities and interests frequently clashed. One solution that was often sought by the town musician of this period was to raise his social status by obtaining an official court appointment, or, if he already had one, by holding on to it. Court music and town music were not, after all, divided into watertight compartments.

When Bach arrived in Leipzig in 1723 he still regarded himself most emphatically as a Court Kapellmeister, especially since he maintained continuing contacts with Cöthen until the death of Duke Leopold in November 1728. We have documents signed by Bach which show that he used his Cöthen title at least until 1729. At about this time (no precise date is known) he also acquired the title of "Kapellmeister to His Highness the Prince of Saxe-Weissenfels", and used both these titles concurrently with those of *Director musices* and Cantor of the Thomasschule. Since July 1733, moreover, he had been appealing to the Court of Saxony in Dresden for a title. This was finally granted on 19 November 1736 and Bach became "Composer to the Royal Court of Poland and to the Elector of Saxony". Bach welcomed the title as a means of commanding some respect from his Leipzig superiors who, he felt, had been belittling him for years. Not that Bach ever lacked self-assurance; his conduct throughout his life makes this quite clear; but he certainly saw it as an extra weapon in his armoury, though not in itself a guarantee of success: he still had to contend with the civic pride, self-confidence and greater power of the Leipzig Council which always, in the last analysis, gave them the upper hand.

Bach's relations with the headmaster, the Town Council and the church authorities may have become progressively more difficult and antagonistic, and the number of his compositions for the church may have decreased, but there were, nevertheless, positive changes being made at this time and new directions being explored as we can tell from his music. It was probably his association with the Collegium Musicum that led to the whole series of concertos for one, two, three, or even four harpsichords. These date from about 1730 and are for the most part re-workings of earlier violin concertos of his own or of other composers. To this period, too, belong the A minor concerto for flute, violin and harpsichord (BWV 1044) and the two D major Overtures (BWV 1086 and 1089). Many of the pieces may have been written for other places, such as Dresden, but this by no means excluded them from performance in Leipzig. We may safely assume that Bach exploited his repertoire from earlier years, above all from his time in Cöthen, for performances with the Collegium Musicum. It is no longer possible to establish the programmes of the concerts given in Zimmermann's coffee-house or garden. Cantatas — of a suitable subject matter and scored for the available forces — were certainly performed there, and there is no doubt that proficient musicians passing through Leipzig, especially the renowned virtuosi, would be invited by Bach to appear with the Collegium. As was the custom at the time, the programmes would have been very varied in content. The works of many other composers would have been played, and works for unaccompanied solo instruments by no means excluded. Chamber music, too, such as Bach played in his own home, was also performed in public.

Bach's six Partitas for harpsichord were printed separately between 1726 and 1730. In 1731 he collected them together into one book (BWV 835–830) which he designated on the title-page as *Clavier-Übung* (*Keyboard Practice*), afterwards adding "Opus 1". In 1735 he followed this by *The Second Part of Keyboard Practice*, consisting of a Concerto after the Italian taste and an Overture after the French manner. After Part One Bach dropped the use of opus numbers, but retained the title *Clavier-Übung*, an indication that he was planning a series that would embrace several different genres. In fact, there were two other parts still to come. The third appeared in 1739 and consisted of "Various Preludes on the Catechism and other hymns, for the organ". Four duets are also included in this collection. Clearly, despite the difference in treatment that had arisen between music for the harpsichord, the clavichord and for the organ, Bach wished to re-establish the affinities between the instruments he had known since his youth. It is clear, too, that Bach's conception of music was as a unified medium, for otherwise the *Clavier-Übung* would never have included two such divergent styles as pieces based on chorales and pieces designed for the congregation's pleasure and refreshment of spirit. The title page of Part Three does, moreover, specify that this music is "for the delight of the mind".

The fourth and last part of the *Clavier-Übung* belongs to the first half of the 1740s, probably between 1742 and 1745. It consists of an "ARIA with manifold variations for two-manual harpsichord". In the nineteenth century it was given the title *Goldberg Variations* (Goldberg was one of Bach's pupils) and the name still persists today. Although Bach was approaching sixty, he continued to plan additions to his *Clavier-Übung*, which, in spite of its span of some fifteen years, we should not regard as complete.

Another collection of keyboard works was roughly contemporary with Part Three of the *Clavier-Übung*. This was the second *Well Tempered Clavier* which Bach finished in 1744. Like the first, written in Cöthen in 1722 it consists of preludes and fugues in every key. The two volumes form a kind of bridge between his time in Cöthen and his later years in Leipzig. The collections also demonstrate the fact that teaching, the activity upon which he had expended so much energy in earlier years, was still important to him. The second *Anna Magdalena Notebook*, begun in 1725, is another obvious example of his interest. Bach's wife herself wrote down the rules of continuo playing as taught by him. These rules are directed primarily at the practical aspects of performance, and theoretical dissertation is largely avoided. The instruction of members of his own family had always had a place in Bach's life. Nearly all the extant material written by Bach for his pupils belongs to the years after 1729.

Although the composition of cantatas of congratulation and homage formed no part of Bach's official duties, he nevertheless wrote about forty during his cantorship, mostly in response to commissions. More often than not he would use the same music for different purposes and sometimes even salvage it for use in the church.

Performances of Bach's great cantatas are, happily, becoming more frequent. For decades the secular cantatas were valued less highly than those written for the church and even their intrinsic musical worth was questioned, but this is an indefensible attitude. The sacred and secular cantatas have different functions, but their musical merit is equal. Even criticisms of the quality of the texts of the secular cantatas should be carefully examined. These texts and those of the sacred cantatas were born of the same poetic and aesthetic mores and belong to the same literary culture, but in the case of the sacred cantatas the language of the Bible and of the traditional scriptural texts imposes a uniquely beautiful style.

Although Bach's musical activities outside the cantorship were obviously considerable — and they increased still further after 1729 — he certainly did not stop writing for the church. The change in emphasis was occasioned for professional reasons and there is absolutely no evidence of any spiritual disaffection whatsoever.

Two great works, both central to Bach's religious oeuvre were, in fact, composed in the 1730s. These are the *Christmas Oratorio* (BWV 248) and the *Mass in B minor* (BWV 232). When Bach presented the Mass in Dresden on 27 July 1733, it consisted only of Kyrie and Gloria. It was an abbreviated form of the Catholic Mass still in use in the Lutheran churches. Bach dedicated it to Frederick Augustus II, King of Poland and Elector of Saxony, in the hope that the Elector might confer on him a title in his court establishment.

The six cantatas in which the story of Christ's birth is told, and which together form the *Christmas Oratorio*, were first performed by Bach and the choir of St Thomas's over Christmas and New Year 1734/5. Bach describes the work on the title page as "An oratorio which was performed during the holy season of Christmas in both the principal churches of Leipzig". A number of individual church cantatas were also written at around this time, some for special occasions, others for the regular Sunday services.

Life in Leipzig was anything but tranquil for Bach and his family. The cantorship was no ivory tower and Bach was kept busy with his duties in the church (which, although they may not have been always fulfilled with the greatest enthusiasm, were constantly proliferating) and his obligations outside it, with his parental duties, and with meeting the many musicians who passed through Leipzig or who had come there specially to visit him. The Bachs' home must have been a scene of constant activity, of comings and goings, of change and even turmoil.

Over the years from the early 1730s to the early 1740s, Bach undertook a considerable number of journeys both for professional and for family reasons. Travel was a habit he had acquired in earlier years, and despite the difficulties it presented, he seems to have enjoyed going to a distant place to play an organ, to perform his own music, or to hear other performers. One might even suppose that Bach regarded travel as a means of self-assertion. In the agreement he signed before assuming the cantorship, Bach had had to accept the stipulation that "Without the permission of the Mayor in office I shall not leave the town". This meant that he had to obtain official leave each time he travelled, and no doubt he did, for the most part. Our knowledge of the journeys that Bach made during his years in Leipzig is probably incomplete, depending as it does on statements made in a totally different context or on written material that has been preserved by chance. Bach went to Weissenfels at least twice, once in February 1729 and again in November 1739. On the first occasion he took part in the musical celebrations for Duke Christian's birthday, the second was probably a family visit to Anna Magdalena's sister who was married to a lawyer at the Weissenfels court, Leberecht Schneider.

Only a few days before he assumed the directorship of the Collegium Musicum, Bach had journeyed to Cöthen. Prince Leopold had died on 19 November 1728, and with his death Bach's ties to Cöthen, which had remained close over the years, had effectively been broken. But on 23 and 24 March, memorial services were held at which Bach performed his Funeral Cantata for the Prince, *Klagt, Kinder, klagt es aller Welt* (BWV 244a). The manuscript of this cantata has been lost since 1818, but we know that nine out of its eleven numbers were taken directly from his *St Matthew Passion*.

Throughout the years in Leipzig Bach nurtured his connections with Dresden; we have documentary evidence of four visits between 1731 and 1741 and can assume that there were others besides. He had always been extremely interested in that city since his 1717 visit, and may even have had thoughts about moving there. The musical life was much more brilliant in Dresden than in Leipzig, there were some exceptionally good musicians in residence, and the scale of music was imposing. There is no doubt that many Dresden musicians made a point of visiting Bach and he was kept well-informed of all that went on there.

On 14 September 1729 Bach played the Silbermann organ in Dresden's Sophien-kirche. He stayed in the town for over a week, performed at court, and probably attended a performance of the opera *Cleofide* by Johann Adolf Hasse (1699–1783) on 13 September. Bach met Hasse, who was the new Hofkapellmeister in Dresden, and his wife Faustina who was a superb singer, and became very friendly with both of them. There were notices about Bach's concerts in the Hamburg and Dresden newspapers at this time and the writers' admiration for Bach is clear. One Dresden paper even printed a little laudatory verse (making a great play of the fact that the word Bach means "brook" in German). The following translation attempts to retain the jingle-like quality of the original:

A rippling brook delights the ear, for sure,
Coursing 'twixt its banks of bush or rock;
But there's a Brook that we esteem much more
for agile hands that wonders great unlock.
When Orpheus played his lute in times gone by,
he drew the beasts to hear him, so they say;
But for our Brook we make a claim more high:
All stand amazed when he but starts to play!

One of the most important trips that Bach made in the 1730s was to Kassel in response to an invitation to test the new organ at the Martinskirche on 22 September 1732 and to inaugurate it on the 28th. As on many of his other trips, he was accompanied by his wife, Anna Magdalena. His travels also took him to Halle in the spring of 1740 and, in August 1741, to Berlin where his son Carl Philipp Emanuel had recently been appointed Court Harpsichordist to Frederick the Great.

Naturally, Bach had helped his sons as much as possible with their careers. When Johann Gottfried Bernhard had auditioned for the post of organist at the Marienkirche in Mühlhausen (Thuringia), his father had accompanied him. He wanted his elder sons to attend university and he had the satisfaction of seeing Wilhelm Friedemann matricu-late at the University of Leipzig in March 1729, followed by his brother Carl Philipp Emanuel in October 1731. The latter afterwards transferred to the University of Frankfurt-on-the-Oder in 1734.

Between 1723 and 1742 Anne Magdalena presented Bach with thirteen children, but, as had been the case in his first marriage, few of the children survived the early years. Birth and death, for the Bachs as for everyone else at this time of extremely high infant mortality, were often inseparable. Of the children born in Leipzig seven died while still very young, several after only a few days:

57. Christmas Oratorio, BWV 248 – opening of the first cantata, autograph.

58. *Faustina Hasse, née Bordoni.*

59. *Johann Adolph Hasse.*

60. *Dresden – stage of the opera house built 1718/19 by Daniel Pöppelmann.*

Christiana Sophia Henrietta (*b.* Spring 1723 – *d.* 29 June 1726)
Gottfried Heinrich (*b.* 26 February 1724)
Christian Gottlieb (baptized 14 April 1725 – *d.* 21 September 1728)
Elisabeth Juliana Friederica (baptized 5 April 1726)
Ernestus Andreas (baptized 30 October 1727 – *d.* 1 November 1727)
Regina Johanna (baptized 10 October 1728 – *d.* 25 April 1733)
Christiana Benedicta (baptized 1 January 1730 – *d.* 4 January 1730)
Christiana Dorothea (baptized 18 March 1731 – *d.* 31 August 1732)
Johann Christoph Friedrich (*b.* 21 June 1732)
Johann August Abraham (baptized 5 November 1733 – *d.* 6 November 1733)
Johann Christian (*b.* 5 September 1735)
Johanna Carolina (baptized 30 September 1737)
Regina Susanna (baptized 22 February 1742)
Johann Gottfried Bernhard, who had been born in Weimar in 1715 of Bach's first marriage, died on 27 May 1739.

A register such as this gives us some idea of how full of incident the Bach household was. Each child brought joy and sorrow, pride and cares into the family. And naturally, the Cantor's house was also the scene of a great deal of musical activity. Bach could not just shut himself away in a room to compose. He had performances to prepare, vocal parts to write out (or to supervise when his copyists, who often included his wife or his sons or pupils, were doing this for him), material to prepare, and his prefects to brief. He also taught at home, giving his private pupils, who included his wife and children, instruction on the clavichord and harpsichord. Social music-making, too, with family and friends was a firmly established feature of life in Leipzig for the Bachs. In a letter to Erdmann, Bach first tells him about the children and then goes on to describe their musical activity: "They are all born musicians and I can assure you that I can indeed form both a vocal and an instrumental ensemble from my family, especially since my present wife has a fine soprano and my eldest daughter does not do badly either."

Although the busy city life of Leipzig made it difficult for Bach to maintain close contact with his relatives in Thuringia, all the evidence suggests that Johann Sebastian was as much of a family man as the rest of the Bach clan. He was loving and generous towards his wife and children — his gifts of flowers and a song-bird to Anna Magdalena demonstrate his affection for her — but this is not to say that he could not be severe and impatient in certain circumstances. He could, and there were times when he even lost his temper. The harmonious family life was frequently threatened by periods of stress caused by worry. One such worry was occasioned by the son Johann Gottfried Bernhard, who, in the spring of 1738, left his post as organist in Sangerhausen — and numerous debts — and disappeared without trace for months.

The old building of the Thomasschule was cramped and inadequate, and in June 1731 the Bach family had to move to alternative lodgings in the Hainstrasse while it was renovated and enlarged by the addition of a further two storeys. It is much to the credit of the Rector, Gesner, that this work which substantially improved the living conditions of the boys, should have been undertaken through his determination to establish the right sort of orderly environment for learning and culture. Music had an important place in Gesner's educational programme, and this no doubt was an important factor that contributed in no small degree to the excellent relations that existed between Cantor and Rector. By April 1732 the Bachs were able to move back into their quarters in the school and on 5 June the newly renovated building was consecrated. For the musical celebration of the event Bach wrote the cantata *Froher Tag, verlangte Stunden* (BWV Anh. 18) to a text by Johann Heinrich Winkler, his colleague at the Thomasschule. The music for this cantata is no longer extant, but it was partially incorporated into other works.

FAVSTINA HASSE
Prima Virtuosa di Camera di S.M. il Re
di Polonia Elettore di Sassonia

GIO: ADOLFO HASSE.
Primo Maestro di Cappella
di Sua Maestà il Re di Polonia
Elettore di Sassonia

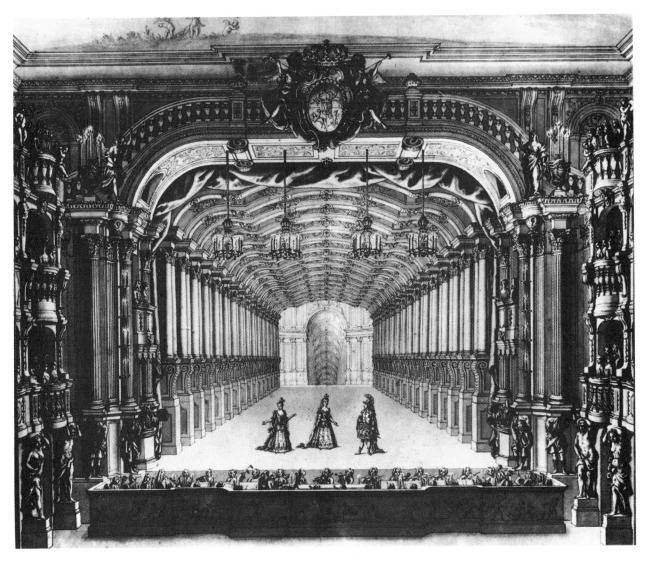

In spite of the disputes that took much of the joy from his work, Cantor and Kapellmeister Bach was now a famous man. As an organist and harpsichordist he had long been respected, as a teacher he was admired and appreciated, as a composer he was acknowledged to be among the greatest, and as an authority on organ-building his opinion was sought time and time again. Many of the disputes in Leipzig may well have stemmed from the fact that this superb musician, who was under no illusion about his own worth, expected to be taken seriously in all matters that affected his expertise and his professional competence. Had he been less stubborn and more willing to give way, his life would have been easier but it is possible that his work would have suffered.

During Bach's lifetime, revolutionary changes were taking place in music, as he himself had pointed out to the Town Council in his "Short Outline" of 1730. The polyphonic style of composition, in which any number of voices were combined and interwoven, was giving way to a style in which a principal melodic line predominated whose expressive power and capacity for nuance reflected the growing spirit of individualism. As we learn from studying the history of music, this was an artistic expression of the emancipation of the middle classes. The result of this process of transformation, which had started at the beginning of the eighteenth century, was the gradual formation of what was to culminate, decades later, in the Viennese classical style. Bach was caught up in this development and was a part of it, as were his great contemporaries such as Vivaldi, Handel, Telemann, Hasse, and Rameau, all of whose work is coloured by it. In comparison to these composers, Bach's musical language, in spite of its modern expressivity, was still very much part of the polyphonic tradition, and although the younger "modernists" of his time certainly regarded him as an undisputed master, they did not consider him an innovator. This is an interesting point that we, who can appreciate the universal quality of his music, see much more clearly than his contemporaries; we do well to bear this in mind as it has an extremely important bearing upon Bach's place and significance in history.

On 14 May 1737 Johann Adolf Scheibe published the sixth issue of his weekly journal *The Critical Musician* in Hamburg. After some phrases of appreciation Scheibe launched into a lengthy critique of Bach's methods of composition:

Finally, Herr . . . is the most eminent of the musicians practising in. . . . He is an extraordinary artist upon the clavier and organ and until now has only encountered one man who could challenge his superiority. I have heard this great man play on several occasions. His ability is amazing and one can hardly conceive how he manages to achieve such amazing dexterity of hand and foot, with such crossings and such extensions that even the widest leaps are accomplished without the intrusion of a single false note and without having to resort to strange contortions of his body.

This great man would be the admiration of the world were he less disposed to deprive his pieces of all naturalness by turgidity and confusion and veil their beauty by artistic excess. Since the dexterity of his own fingers is the standard by which he judges, he requires a similar dexterity from singers with their throats and instrumentalists with their instruments to achieve that which he can produce upon the keyboard. But this is impossible. Every little grace and embellishment that belongs to this style of playing, he writes out in full, which not only takes away from the beauty of the harmony but also conceals the melody. Every voice must work together with the others and all have an equal measure of difficulty, so that one is unable to recognize any leading voice. In short, he is in music what Herr von Lohenstein once was in poetry. The turgidity of their style has led them both away from the natural towards the artificial, away from the elevated towards the obscure. In both cases one admires the hard work and exceptional effort, which are however applied in vain, for they are struggling against nature.

Scheibe, the son of a Leipzig organ builder, was born in 1708. He studied law and philosophy in his native city and developed a deep interest in music. In 1729 he was an unsuccessful candidate for the post of organist at the Thomaskirche, and in 1736 he went to Hamburg. He had grown up with the ideas of the Enlightenment and had been much affected by the Leipzig literary theorist and poet, Johann Christoph Gottsched. For years he had been part of the same musical scene in Leipzig as Bach himself, but his own tastes were for the new, predominantly melodic style, so although he may have felt some resentment towards Bach over his failure at the Thomaskirche, his strictures were not inspired by personal pique but rather by a radical change of musical thinking that, because its influence was constantly growing, Bach must have experienced from other quarters, for instance in the musical development of his own sons. Scheibe's polemic shows that the world in which Bach lived was by no means a unified one free from conflict and dissension; this did not only apply to music, but it also shows that besides not having recognized the complexity of Bach's music, he had not seen the features in it that were new.

Bach did not trouble to reply personally to Scheibe's attack. He probably felt little inclination to engage in a verbal feud in which the young and eloquent Scheibe might have got the better of him, and which might have invited further criticism. Basically, subjective attitudes towards music played such a decisive role in the aesthetic dispute that it could never be settled by polemics. Besides, eight years previously Bach had composed a cantata, possibly for performance in Zimmerman's coffee-house, in which he had tackled in his own way the problem of the simple and the complex in relation to beauty. This was *Geschwinde, ihr wirbelnden Winde: Der Streit zwischen Phoebus und Pan*, ("Swift, ye whirling winds: The quarrel between Phoebus and Pan", BWV 201). Picander's poem had invited an almost operatic representation of a singing contest, and Bach had been able to express a fundamental musical problem in an amusing and entertaining way.

All the same, Scheibe's attack cannot have left him unmoved, especially since he had been struggling for years for a better understanding of the principles underlying his music. At the beginning of January 1738, Bach's friend Johann Abraham Birnbaum (1702–48), a lecturer in rhetoric at the University of Leipzig, published a defence of Bach entitled: "Unbiased comments on a dubious passage in Issue VI of *The Critical Musician*". Scheibe in turn defended himself repeatedly. Bach may have possibly initiated Birnbaum's response; he certainly knew about it. Naturally, no real solution could be found in this way, because questions of musical taste are not susceptible to solution in pamphlets, depending as they do upon social and historical conditions. Bach was to be drawn once more into a dispute over the nature of music, however, in the last months of his life. The Freiburg headmaster, Johann Gottlieb Biedermann (1705–72), had published a school programme in May 1749 in which he drew extremely dubious conclusions about the corrupting influence of music and defamatory comments about the whole musical profession.[8] Widespread reaction to Biedermann's remarks even affected Bach, who was stirred into action not only by his memories of Scheibe but on account of his bitter experience with his own headmaster, Joh. August Ernesti. Above all, he was motivated by his self-esteem as a musician. He arranged for Gottlieb Schröter, an organist in Nordhausen, and, like him, a member of Mizler's Musical Society, to write and publish a review. However, this review appeared in an altered form and caused a lot of trouble. In connection with the Biedermann affair — and probably at Bach's instigation — another performance was given in Leipzig of Bach's cantata, *Phoebus und Pan*.

The more we know about Bach's life in Leipzig, the more clearly we see that it was a time of dynamic social activity for Bach. His personal connections were reaching out ever further and in many different directions. This continued throughout the remainder of his life. Bach came into contact with a great many people through his position, through his

61. Left: Johann Adolphe Scheibe: "Critischer Musicus", Leipzig 1745, title page of the reprint with the 1737 attack on Bach.

62. Right: Johann Abraham Birnbaum: first page of defence of Bach against Scheibe's attack, 1739.

Johann Adolph Scheibens,

Königl. Dänis. Capellmeisters,

Critischer MUSIKUS.

Neue,

vermehrte und verbesserte Auflage.

Leipzig,

bey Bernhard Christoph Breitkopf, 1745.

Dem

Hochedlen Herrn,

Herrn Johann Sebastian Bachen,

Sr. Königl. Maj. in Pohlen, und Churfürstl. Durchl. zu Sachsen hochbestalltem Hofcompositeur und Capellmeister, wie auch Directorn der Musik und Cantorn an der Thomasschule in Leipzig,

widmet

diese Ihn selbst angehende Blätter

mit vieler Ergebenheit

der Verfasser.

HORATIVS.

Quid verum atque decens curo, et rogo, et omnis in hoc sum.

Derjenige soll noch gebohren werden, der das ganz besondere Glück haben wird, allen zu gefallen. Es ist zwar nicht zu läugnen; einen Menschen, der als ein Inbegriff aller Vollkommenheiten, allgemeinen Beyfall zu erhalten würdig wäre, werden wir in einer Welt, welcher die Unvollkommenheit nur allzueigen, vergebens erwarten. Allein wir haben billig Ursache, zufrieden zu seyn, wenn bey der unzertrennlichen Verbindung des

Ggg 2   Guten

work as composer, teacher, and practising musician, and not least through his family obligations. There was no other musician in Leipzig of remotely the same status, influence, and responsibility. The cantorship brought him into daily contact with the school, the Church authorities, and also the Town Council and its various administrative bodies. The university was also vital to Bach's work, not as an employer but as the source of students for the Collegium Musicum. His links with Dresden became stronger over the years; he made several visits to the town and his home, a regular port of call for all musicians, became most especially so for those from Dresden. Through the musical connections that he had built up all through his life, and his growing reputation, he was greatly in demand as a teacher for young musicians. Numerous organists, cantors, and future Kapellmeister came from among the ranks of his pupils, and their certificates and testimonials — plus the names and addresses on such documents — are a valuable source of information on Bach's contacts.

No real understanding of this side of Bach's life is possible without reference to his ancestry and family tradition with its roots in Thuringia and the Thuringian mentality. The Thuringian Bachs may be described as friendly, predominantly good-tempered and open-minded, though with a love of tradition. They were always ready to help each other in both family and professional matters, but in doing so they never forgot their own interests. Their way of life was modest, since Thuringia at this time boasted little in the way of material and economic development. The Thuringians were predominantly Lutherans, and the code of ethics that they derived from their faith was as characteristic of them as a certain peasant cunning by which they contrived to turn practical considerations to their advantage. The Thuringian peasants' overriding sense of the value of freedom and justice was demonstrated in their struggles under Thomas Müntzer. The character of the Thuringian people must owe something at least to the Thuringian landscape with its mountains and valleys, forests, watercourses and meadows, its particular combination of gentle loveliness and raw desolation.

While working in Leipzig, Bach naturally maintained contact with his family and also extended his connections to include that of his second wife. His family circle was widened still further as his children married and established their own households, although here the links became more tenuous. And we should not forget the innumerable times Bach and his wife were invited to act as godparents to the children of friends or relatives, for each of these invitations implies a connection of some consequence.

As Bach's circle of relations, friends, and acquaintances increased, so did the amount of time that he had to spend in attending to it. Letters had to be drafted and written, questions asked and answered, family problems solved, visits organized, advice given and instructions issued. The older he got, the more difficult Bach found coping with all this; perhaps the problems themselves became more complicated. Eventually, in autumn 1737, he engaged his cousin Johann Elias Bach (1705–55) as private secretary and tutor to the younger children, supplementing the work that Anna Magdalena had done for him up to this time. Elias had studied at the university of Jena, but had been forced to leave for financial reasons. He helped his cousin with his correspondence for five years, managing also to resume his theological studies in 1739. There are about 250 letters still extant in drafts in his hand. He left the Bach household in autumn 1742, but kept in contact for several years and was clearly at pains to demonstrate his friendly feelings towards his relative. In a letter of 2 November 1748, Bach thanks Elias for sending him a small barrel of wine, a third of whose contents had unfortunately been lost. Although Bach is naturally well pleased to receive wine of such quality, he has to ask his cousin not to send presents of this kind in future because the freight charge was sixteen groschen, the delivery two groschen, payment to the excise officer two groschen, local tax five groschen and three pfennigs, and general tax three groschen, and "my cousin can judge for himself that as each measure cost me nearly five groschen, this is too expensive a present".

There is every indication that Bach was practical in family matters. The harshness of everyday life, the cruel juxtaposition of life and death through high infant and child mortality, the still primitive standards of hygiene, the relative simplicity of food, clothing, and accommodation, all led to an attitude that was unsentimental, to the directness and clarity that we also find in his music. When Cousin Elias asked for a copy of the "Prussian Fugue", we find Bach requesting the price, one thaler, in advance.

In the last decade of his life, Bach's duties as Cantor diminished. From 1740 the pupils at St Thomas's were taught music theory by a teacher specifically appointed for the job, and many of the choir rehearsals and performances were conducted by the prefects who worked under the Cantor's guidance. There were probably several reasons for this, including Bach's absences from Leipzig, his possible indisposition and, in all probability, his decreasing interest in the post which he had now held for twenty years. The stream of new cantatas had long dried up and he relied much more frequently on repeating old ones or using the works of other composers. He had given up the direction of the Collegium Musicum from March 1737 until October 1739, but then resumed it until the early 1740s. From 1741 there were reports about forming a concert society, which became the Grosses Concert in 1743, replacing the Collegium Musicum and led eventually to the Leipzig Gewandhaus concerts. The part that Bach played in these developments will some day be revealed by research still in progress. Earlier suppositions that he was unconcerned about these matters and even preferred to withdraw from public life, are probably mistaken.

A whole series of events, both in family and professional life, made Bach's last years a turbulent time. International politics, too, intruded upon the life of the Cantor. When Frederick the Great invaded Austria with the object of extending his dominion over the mineral-rich region of Silesia, Saxony threw in its lot with Austria and was defeated in 1742. Towards the end of the Second Silesian War on 30 November 1745, Leipzig was occupied by Prussian troops, and when the Treaty of Dresden was signed on 25 December,

63. *Surrender of the city of Leipzig to the Prussian troops on 30.11.1745*

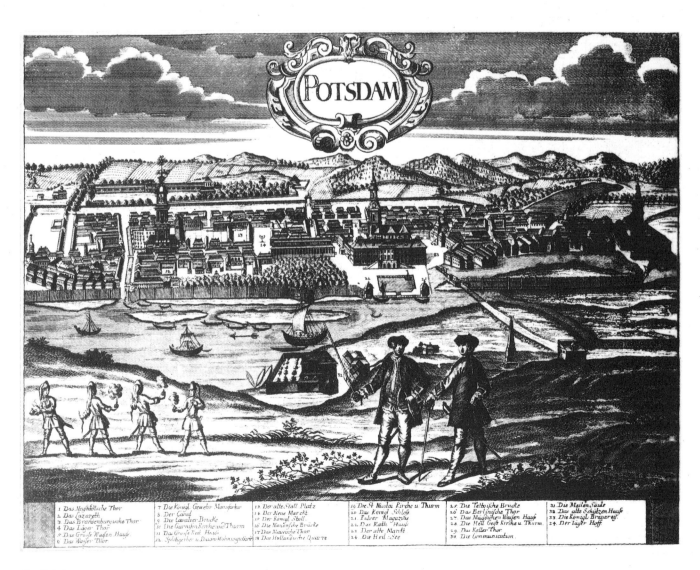

64. *Potsdam*

not only Silesia but Saxony became a part of Prussia and Bach was therefore a subject of the Prussian king. His son, Carl Philipp Emanuel, who had been in Frederick's service for years, saw this as a golden opportunity for his father and obtained an invitation for him to appear at the court in Potsdam. Bach had visited his son previously in August 1741, but since then Carl Philipp had married and founded his own branch of the family in Berlin. Well aware of his sovereign's musical inclinations, he seems to have tried to bring his father to Frederick's attention several times. This time he succeeded, and at the beginning of May 1747 Bach travelled with his eldest son, Wilhelm Friedemann, to Potsdam. On 7 and 8 May he performed before Frederick on the harpsichord and organ. But the sixty-two-year-old Bach did not belong to the same musical world as the thirty-five-year-old king who had been captivated by the Italian instrumental style with its emphasis on cantabile melody. Frederick may well have admired Bach's masterly playing and his command of a disciplined and carefully wrought style, but to the young sovereign the old master must have seemed outdated and out of touch with the elegance and lightness of the new style, his fame embodying the musical past rather than the present.

65. *Frederick II (the Great), King of Prussia.*

66. *Potsdam – the palace.*

When Bach left Potsdam he presumably went on to Berlin to visit Carl Philipp Emanuel, his wife, and their eighteen-month-old son Johann Adam. On his return to Leipzig he composed a work in several movements based on a theme suggested by the king upon which he had improvised variations on the Silbermann harpsichord in Potsdam. This became *Musical Offering* (BWV 1079). Bach himself had it printed, provided a dedication to Frederick the Great, had it expensively bound, and sent it as a "Dutiful offering of thanks" to Potsdam. The king neither acknowledged receipt of the work nor offered any payment. Perhaps his interest in Johann Sebastian had lasted only as long as his visit.

A few weeks after his return from Potsdam Bach joined the Society of Musical Sciences, founded by Lorenz Mizler (1711–78) in 1738. Mizler had studied the harpsichord and composition with Bach in Leipzig and had shown himself an apt and talented pupil. After graduating he became a professor of Mathematics, Philosophy, and Music at the University of Leipzig. Mizler was a man of the Enlightenment who approached music from the rational and scientific points of view, and he hoped that his learned society would achieve its aims by attracting members from among the leading musical figures. He had a certain measure of success, for on its membership rolls we find the names of Georg Philipp Telemann, Gottfried Heinrich Stölzel, George Frideric Handel, and Carl Heinrich Graun. And now, finally, after repeated efforts, his respected teacher Johann Sebastian Bach added his name to the list. The statutes of membership required that Bach should submit a composition; thus, in the 1746 portrait by Gottlob Haussman (the most significant portrait of Bach that has survived, reproduced here on the frontis-

67. *The Art of Fugue, BWV 1080, first page of the autograph.*

piece), he is shown holding the manuscript of a triple canon in his right hand. The canonic variations on the Christmas song "Vom Himmel hoch" (BWV 769) were also submitted, and Bach probably presented the manuscripts of both these elaborate works to the society when he became a member. Recent research has also associated the *Musical Offering* and the later, unfinished *Art of Fugue*, BWV 1080, with Mizler's society. Although it would seem that Bach had little inclination towards theoretical reasoning and mathematical abstraction (the *Nekrolog* tells us this much), he must have viewed his entry into the Society as an excellent opportunity to display his art and his experience before a circle of proven experts. Perhaps the idea that Bach became something of a hermit in his last years has its roots in this, and yet the works of his old age are much more than exercises in theory: the art in them is alive and forward-looking. Taking the totality of Bach's works and looking at them from a historical standpoint, we can see a clear progression towards an ever greater compression or condensation starting with the *Clavier-Übung*, continuing with Book II of the *Well Tempered Clavier*, the *Musical Offering*, and the Canonic Variations, and culminating in *The Art of Fugue*. This last great work put the seal on a lifetime's experience.

During the last years of his life, even Bach himself had to come to terms with the fact that he belonged to an older generation. His sons, Wilhelm Friedemann, Carl Philipp Emanuel and (from 1750) Johann Christoph Friedrich, held eminent posts in Halle, Berlin/Potsdam and Bückeburg; Johann Christian, born in 1735, was showing great musical promise; his son-in-law Christoph Altnickol had obtained a position in Naumburg, and his pupils were already achieving success in many different places from Altenburg to Freiburg, from Leipzig and Schweinfurt, from Berlin to Sondershausen. His relationships with his sons were not always smooth. None of them failed to appreciate his greatness, at least in a general way, but parental relationships were still problematical. Their musical taste was that of the younger generation and they wanted to strike out on their own rather than stand in the shadow of their great father. Nor did they want to submit to the stresses and strains of conventional appointments. Each in his own way achieved a measure of social and artistic emancipation, but theirs was a time of transition. No longer would it be possible for any one man to dominate the heights as their father had done, free to select from the past and the present, commanding and consolidating a vast range of musical experience. Their work was tied into the Enlightenment; it was perforce less comprehensive than that of their father but more individually expressive,

S. Johannis Kirche mit dem
neu gebauten Thurm

70. Leipzig –
St John's Church and
cemetery.

and with them lay the responsibility for taking the next step towards the musical apotheosis of Viennese Classicism.

Bach had turned sixty in 1745, just two months before the Prussians moved into Leipzig. He was an old man by the standards of his time. The average life expectation at that time was fifty-six years. He had probably paid little consistent attention to his health (who could in those days?) but we have no biological evidence of serious or recurring illnesses. Eye trouble is, however, mentioned in the *Nekrolog*: "His sight, somewhat weak by nature, had become even weaker through his unparalleled zest for study, at which, especially in his youth, he would spend whole nights, and in his last years this brought about an affliction of the eyes." His eyesight eventually deteriorated to such an extent that he could no longer continue to produce work at the same rate as before. By the spring of 1750 his eyes were so bad that he was given the choice of going blind (and having to give up his work) or having an operation. At that time an English eye surgeon, John Taylor, was performing public operations before a select audience in Leipzig, and Bach entrusted himself to him, putting hopes for help above any doubts that he may have had. He underwent two operations, one on 1 April, the second on the 4th. At first there were premature announcements of a success (possibly in the interests of Taylor's reputation), but these were later proved untrue. The *Nekrolog* takes up the story:

Not only could he no longer use his eyes, but the whole of his otherwise healthy system was by this and by harmful medicaments and suchlike, completely over-thrown: thus, for six whole months he was continually ill. Ten days before his death his eyes suddenly seemed to improve, so that one morning he found that he could see quite well and could endure the light again. But a few hours later he suffered a stroke; this was followed by a raging fever, to which, in spite of every possible medical attention on the part of two of the most skilful physicians in Leipzig, he succumbed on 28 July 1750, just after a quarter to nine in the evening, in the sixty-sixth year of his life, when, by the grace of his Redeemer, he quietly and peacefully departed.

An obituary published in Leipzig on 31 July announced his death briefly and factually:

Last Tuesday, the 28th of this month, the death occurred in this very town of the celebrated musician Herr Johann Sebastian Bach, Court Composer to the King of Poland and the Elector of Saxony, Kapellmeister to His Highness the Prince of Saxe-Weissenfels and to the court of Anhalt-Cöthen, Director of the Chori musici and Cantor at the Thomasschule in this town, in his sixty-sixth year as the unfor-tunate result of a badly performed eye-operation by a well-known English eye-surgeon. The loss of this uncommonly skilled man will be mourned by all connoisseurs of music.

He was buried on 31 July in St John's cemetery.

71. *Orgelbüchlein – title page of autograph.*

Organ and Keyboard Music

Bach's interest in keyboard instruments began when he was a child and continued to the end of his life. In both cases the instruments had a duel role in the music of their time: they provided the basso continuo for many different kinds of music, and at the same time were fast developing as solo instruments with a repertoire of their own. As we have already seen, Bach himself was one of the most notable performers of his time upon the organ and harpsichord. The organ was, of course, his prime instrument, but of the other keyboard instruments he had a special fondness for the clavichord. Forkel tells us:

> Best of all he liked to play upon the clavichord; the harpsichord, although best suited for a different kind of performance, had not enough character for him, and the pianoforte was insufficiently developed in his lifetime and too coarse to satisfy him. Thus he considered that the clavichord was the best instrument to study upon as well as being generally the best for private musical entertainment. He found it the most suitable for the performance of his most refined inspirations and doubted that any harpsichord or pianoforte could bring out the many gradations of tone he required as well as the clavichord, which, in spite of its weak tone, is, on a small scale, extremely flexible.

Forkel's biography of Bach has the advantage of drawing upon first-hand reports from people who had known Bach personally, and contains a great deal of material supplied by Bach's son Carl Philipp Emanuel. In Chapter II he relates a famous story about the young Johann Sebastian when he was receiving his first lessons on the keyboard from his elder brother Johann Christoph in Ohrdruf. Inexplicably denied access to a book containing music by some of the most famous composers of the day — men like Froberger, Fischer, Kerll, Pachelbel, Buxtehude, Bruhns and Böhm — he secretly copied it out at night, painstakingly transcribing the compositions into an exercise book by the light of the moon. The fact that his brother eventually found out about this clandestine activity and confiscated the exercise book is not really important; the music was now in his head anyway, and twenty elder brothers could not have removed it from there. Much more important to us is this astonishing proof of the boy's obsession with music. The story also demonstrates clearly that his abilities as a performer must have been developing very rapidly indeed, for no child would think of expending such effort on the acquisition of compositions which he did not expect to be able to play himself within the foreseeable future.

Little is known about his early life, but his first compositions and his first employment as a professional musician clearly presuppose an intimate familiarity with the organ and harpsichord. As a child in Eisenach he would have heard his uncle Johann Christoph, a very able and respected organist, and when he went to live in Ohrdruf at the age of ten, he probably began to play the instrument himself. Interest in the construction of keyboard instruments and organs was an important corollary to playing them, and throughout his life he was called upon for his expert opinion of new samples of the instrument-builders' craft. The tuning of an instrument, the techniques associated with its performance, and its range of possibilities were all matters about which he had a thoroughly professional fund of knowledge, and naturally, when it came to composing and performing on them this served him well.

The writers of the *Nekrolog* have this to say about Bach's abilities as a performer:

Since no one has ever suggested more than the merest possibility of there existing better organists and clavier players, we can boldly venture to claim that our Bach was the best we have ever had. Many a famous man may have achieved much in polyphony upon these instruments; does this necessarily mean that he was as skilled, and did his hands and feet possess that skill which our Bach possessed? Whoever had the opportunity of hearing him and others, will echo this doubt if not carried away by prejudice. And whoever considers the works that Bach wrote for clavier and organ — and himself performed, as everyone knows, with such perfection — will not find much to quarrel with in the above statement. How strange, how new, how expressive, how beautiful were his ideas when he improvised! How fully were they realized! Every finger was employed equally. Each was capable of the utmost refinement and accuracy in performance. So well did he finger a piece that nothing was awkward, and even the most difficult feats were performed with fluent facility. Before him, even the most celebrated of German and foreign keyboard players had largely neglected the thumb, so his use of it was the more praiseworthy. With his two feet he could play upon the pedals passages which many a skilful player would have found hard enough to perform with five fingers. He did not only understand the art of playing upon the organ, of combining the stops in the most effective manner and allowing each stop to speak with its own individuality to perfection, but he also knew about the construction of the organ inside out. This he demonstrated upon one occasion especially, when examining the new organ of the church not far from where his earthly remains now lie. The organ-builder responsible for this instrument was a man nearing the end of his life. The examination was one of the most severe, perhaps, that had ever been undertaken, so that when he gave the instrument his full approval, the verdict did no little credit either to the organ-builder or (because of certain special circumstances) to Bach himself.

No one knew better than Bach how to plan the disposition of a new organ or how to judge it. But in spite of all the knowledge about organs, he never, as he himself used to complain, had at his continual disposal any really large or beautiful organ. This fact has robbed us of many fine and never-to-be-heard compositions for the organ which he would otherwise have written down for assuredly they were in his head. He knew how to tune a harpsichord so accurately that every key sounded beautiful and pleasant. He knew of no key that, because of its impurity of tuning, should be avoided. Not to mention his many other talents!

Bach's own musical development gives us the best indication of which organ masters and which regional traditions had the most important influence upon him. Certainly the older members of his own family in Thuringia exercised an important and early influence. The most significant of these was Johann Christoph Bach, the court and town organist in Eisenach whom Johann Sebastian later described as "a profound musician", and whose compositions were still in his nephew's repertoire during his time in Leipzig. In the broadest sense, Bach's mastery of the organ was the culmination of a tradition which had been developing for more than a hundred years and encompassed Italy (Frescobaldi), Southern Germany (Froberger), the Netherlands (Sweelinck) and North Germany (Scheidt). Other important influences upon him were Pachelbel, who worked in both Erfurt and Gotha, Georg Böhm (Lüneburg), Jan Adams Reinken (Hamburg) and Dietrich Buxtehude (Lübeck). In the music of Johann Sebastian Bach, all these various traditions fuse, are focused, and given new life.

Although organs, because of their intimate association with sacred music, were invariably situated in churches, their repertoire was by no means limited to a liturgical function. Nevertheless, it was inevitable that a significant proportion of this repertoire did develop from the part the organ played in the Protestant church service, particularly from the chorale, which had had an educational as well as a liturgical function since the time of Luther as his teachings were enshrined in their texts. Bach arranged over 300 chorales, here achieving the heights of four-part writing. The chorales form one group of Bach's compositions for organ, his freely-composed works, another. In the first group his inventiveness was bounded by the texts and the existing melodies, but in the second he could give his fantasy free rein and allow himself a virtuosic style of concerto-like richness.

In the chorale-based organ works, Bach treats the chorale melody as the starting point for elaborations which he had adapted from previous masters of the organ and which he went on to enrich in his own unique way. The main chorale forms (closely linked and not always distinguishable from each other) were the Prelude, Partita, Fantasia, Fugue, and Variations. Bach had become familiar with Partita form from the work of Georg Böhm, organist of the Johanniskirche in Lüneburg.

The following four chorale partitas (c.1700), although they cannot be more precisely dated, are the earliest of his extant compositions:

Partite diverse sopra Christ, der du bist der helle Tag, BWV 766
Partite diverse sopra O Gott, du frommer Gott, BWV 767
Partite diverse sopra Sei gegrüsst, Jesu gütig, BWV 768
Partite diverse sopra Ach, was soll ich Sünder machen?, BWV 770.

The number of sections contained in each varies from seven to eleven. The first section presents the chorale melody as a four- or five-part theme which is subsequently elaborated upon in a series of ingenious variations. By the time he went to Weimar, Bach had moved away from the chorale partita and it played no further part in his composition.

The chorale prelude is a form of the utmost importance. Here the chorale melody is presented, whole or in sections, within a freely-composed framework that reflects the poetic, figurative, or abstract elements of the chorale text. Bach wrote a great many of these, and they are a vital key to his thought, both religious and musical. Writing about the preludes contained in the *Orgelbüchlein*, Albert Schweitzer described them as "the dictionary of his musical language, the key to our comprehension of Bach's music in general". It was the chorale preludes that had prompted the reproach administered to Bach by the Consistory in Arnstadt when he was only twenty years old. His embellishments of the chorale had evidently given rise to a certain unease on the part of the good folk of Arnstadt, and probably to the members of the not outstandingly proficient choir, too, with whom Bach was already unpopular. The reason for this uneasiness was that the singing of the chorale became much more difficult when the melody was elaborately ornamented; hence the intervention of the Consistory whose responsibility was towards the maintenance of standards in the interests of all. The fact that Bach came into such a conflict with his superiors signals nothing less than the first stirrings of artistic independence.

There were no hard and fast criteria that applied to the writing of chorale preludes.

The manner in which the theme was quoted and used and the length of the interludes between the sections of the melody was left entirely to the discretion of the composer. Bach's techniques can be illustrated by reference to Prelude No. 20 of the *Orgelbüchlein*, the collection which Bach began in Weimar and never completed. Taking the chorale text "O Lamm Gottes unschuldig" (BWV 618), Bach translates the thoughts and emotions expressed into musical terms above the chorale melody, the *cantus firmus*. Two elements are here combined, adherence to the chorale tradition and its theological basis, and an extremely "modern" style that aims to express a profound truthfulness. The text of the chorale is as follows:

> O Lamb of God, tho' stainless
> Slain upon the Tree,
> Unmov'd was Thy blest patience
> By scorn and contumely.
> All sins Thou borest there
> That we might not despair.

72. Orgelbüchlein – "O Lamm Gottes, unschuldig", BWV 618, autograph.

73. Arnstadt – Bach's organ console in the New Church.

The chorale melody is presented as a canon at the fifth. The canon is the strictest form of melodic imitation, and in its logic, its implacable order and sternness, are reflected the ineluctibility of the will of God as the orderer of destiny.

in Canone alla Quinta

The subjective aspect now becomes more important, the more emotive treatment evoking the cruel death on the Cross, the innocence of the sacrifice, the patient and unprotesting acceptance of the burden of sin, the mercy shown to all sinners. There is grief here and a sorrowful acknowledgement of guilt in which Bach participates; he surrounds the melody sung in canon with an aura of lamentation, expressed in a continuous succession of sighs:

This kind of musical presentation should not be considered programmatic in the Romantic sense of the word. The lament is quite unsentimental and more concerned with psychological truth than with picture-painting. There is a sense of realism as well, however. Bach was to develop this treatment of the text in his later vocal works.

The chorale prelude was to remain Bach's favourite form for elaborating on the chorale melody. Although there was a lull in his activity as an organist after he had left Weimar for Cöthen, Leipzig saw a resurgence of organ composition and four collections of chorale preludes were eventually published there. These were *Clavier-Übung III* (1739), the six *Schübler Chorales* (1746), the *Canonic Variations on "Vom Himmel hoch"* (1746) and the posthumously published *Eighteen Chorales of various kinds* (1750).

The title page of the first edition of *Clavier-Übung III* reads:

Third Part
of the
CLAVIER-ÜBUNG
consisting
of
various preludes
on
the Catechism and other Hymns
for the organ:
for the delight and edification
of amateurs and especially those
who are connoisseurs of these things
composed by
JOHANN SEBASTIAN BACH
Court composer to the King of Poland
and Elector of Saxony, Capellmeister
and Director Chori Musici Lipsiensis
Published by the Author

The title page covers most of the contents of the *Clavier-Übung*, but not all. We are given no indication of the careful overall design of the work which begins with a prelude in E flat major for organ (BWV 552,1), follows the chorale preludes with four duets for two-manual organ or harpsichord (BWV 802–805), and concludes with a five-part fugue again for organ (BWV 552,2). This very solid, if subtle, framework within which ostensibly heterogeneous elements are bound together has given rise to many speculative interpretations. The reference on the title page to the Catechism indicates that the collection contains the six Lutheran chorales that the Catechism includes. The Kyrie and Gloria would follow these six chorales in the German order of service. Each hymn appears in two versions, one for organ with pedals and one for manuals only, suitable for the harpsichord. Despite the organization of the work as a whole, Bach gives no indication whether he intended this Third Part of the *Clavier-Übung* to be played as a cycle or as separate pieces, though analogy with Parts I and II would suggest the latter. On the other hand, the overall shape of the work, linking as it does chorale and non-liturgical music within a particular frame, indicates the presence of some large-scale unifying concept.

The eagerness that Bach felt about collecting and publishing his works for the organ is also evidenced by the publication in 1746 of the *Six Chorales*. These were taken primarily from cantatas and all but one are transcriptions rather than works specifically composed for the organ. Whereas in the other chorale preludes the melody of the chorale is elaborated upon in variations or with figurations — as is the case in the *Clavier-Übung* — in the *Six Chorales* the ritornello (the recurring prelude, interlude, and postlude) assumes a particularly important role, forming a poetic context for the chorale melody. These are sometimes extended into twelve-bar sections, creating a concertante relationship between the ritornello and the chorale passages:

The collection of eighteen chorales, upon which Bach was still working at the very end of his life, and whose last pieces had to be dictated to his son-in-law Altnickol, are in the main pieces which go back to his time in Weimar. Their workmanship and power of expression endow them with a richness, variety and breadth which have never been matched in this genre by any other composer.

The *Canonic variations on the Christmas song "Vom Himmel hoch"* (BWV 769) which were submitted by Bach upon entering Lorenz Mizler's society in summer 1747, summarize his canonic treatment of the organ chorale in a way that is both practical and theoretical. In the canon Bach deploys within the narrowest confines a creative freedom that allows him to have all four melodic lines playing both with and against one another within the space of three bars. The prayer for divine guidance that Bach uttered with the words "Jesu Juva" written so often above his sacred music was answered by an ever-growing mastery of his art and a unique power of human expression through music.

1–4 = Liedmelodie; 1a = Umkehrung von 1; 1b = Verkleinerung von 1; 3a = Variante von 3

Chorale-based and freely-composed organ music had developed side by side. In the seventeenth century a whole group of genres appeared, such as the canzona, fantasia, prelude, ricercar, and fugue, for the most part all based on variation and imitation. In North Germany the virtuosic element was given its head. This was a direct result of the technical improvements that such instrument-makers as Schnitger, Hildebrandt, Silbermann, and Werckmeister had made. Development was reflected, *inter alia*, in the toccata, whose fantasia-like form, characterized by an improvisatory style, made it an excellent vehicle for display. Passage work, dynamic variety, changes of registration, chordal sections, showed off the capabilities of the instrument as well as the skill of the performer, the art of the composer, and the craft of the organ-builder. Towards the end of the seventeenth century, fugal sections became more frequent in the toccata, as indeed they already had in the canzona. The three-part structure of toccata — fugue — toccata developed into the two-part structure of prelude and fugue which was at the very heart of freely-composed organ music from around 1700 and was that preferred by Bach. The occasional substitution of a toccata or fantasia for the prelude did not alter the basic form.

The essential element in the successful combination of these two movements is that of contrast. The prelude (or toccata or fantasia) is characterized by spontaneity, improvisation, subjectivity, and virtuosic brilliance. The fugue, on the other hand, demands adherence to the principles of counterpoint and imposes such requirements as order and proportion, design, scholarly learning, and fine workmanship. By such a juxtaposition of styles, new possibilities emerged for contrasting sequences, linking them, and dividing them in such a way that a new field of individual expression was opened up. In fact it was this very coupling of prelude and fugue that led directly to the structural principle of development which was to evolve particularly in the other instrumental forms of sonata, the concerto and the symphony.

Bach had come into contact early with the Italian concerto and had absorbed the sonata's potential for the development of themes and motives. His meeting with the elderly Dietrich Buxtehude was also extremely important, but the young Bach was too deeply entrenched in the Thuringian traditions for there to have been any possibility

74. *Mühlhausen – Divi Blasii, interior with the organ completed in 1959 to Bach's specifications.*

that he would develop into a composer for the organ on the lines of the North German style. Nevertheless, the brilliance of this particular style, the individuality of its virtuosity, and its capacity for imaginative musical expression must have been a great stimulus to his own genius, perhaps even a confirmation of his own tendencies. Even as early as this, Bach's characteristic capacity for synthesis seems to have been well developed. Hence we find that his early compositions are marked by a boldness of approach, by an ability to preserve the old and explore the new at the same time. From the unusual demands that he makes on pedal technique, we can deduce that his own dexterity must have been extraordinary, and this is combined with an almost wayward fantasy.

Apart from even earlier pieces, there are compositions for the organ dating from the end of Bach's time in Weimar which are so grand in conception and concerto-like in their virtuosity that the audience is swept along by them. These far surpass any previous models. The most famous of them is undoubtedly the Toccata and Fugue in D minor (BWV 565):

Two well-established principles are here combined: that of quoting sections of the fugue in the toccata, and that of thematic association between them:

The effect of the whole work is, however, that of a majestic river sweeping along and overflowing its banks. The work is in three parts, the toccata returning at the end of the fugue to recapitulate the drama of the opening. The toccata fulfils all the requirements of the form, but instead of simply fitting into a preconceived pattern, it emancipates itself. The fugue echoes the sequence of intervals from the toccata but transforms them into strings of semiquavers. Such is the dramatic contrast between the two sections that these similarities are not immediately obvious. The young Bach was already displaying the creative powers of the great musician. In this piece we see the originality of thought which led Bach to abandon the traditional chorale prelude and strike out in new and unprecedented directions.

In Weimar, Bach had the opportunity of learning new works by the Italian masters and discovering the principles of the contemporary concerto, which was being eagerly adopted in Germany and becoming highly fashionable. From the Italians, especially Vivaldi, he learned how to write flexibly for the orchestra and soloists, how to contrast alternating sections, about the compression and extension of themes, and the style of composition that centres on a single melodic line. While in Weimar, Bach and his cousin Johann Gottfried Walther, the town organist, transcribed several concertos, particularly those for violin with string orchestra, for the organ and harpsichord. They had probably been requested to do this by the young Prince Johann Ernst, who wrote music, studied with Walther and possibly with Bach too, and died in 1715 at the age of nineteen.

Throughout his life Bach was always eager to learn from the music of other composers, and what could be more natural than that he should use his opportunities in Weimar to widen his knowledge and build upon the experience that he had already gained in North Germany? He took a great interest not only in modern Italian orchestral and chamber works, but also in the compositions of earlier French and Italian masters. The organ works that he wrote in Weimar clearly show these influences and some themes, for instance, are borrowed directly from Italian works. The considerable number of non-liturgical pieces that he wrote for the organ in Weimar bear witness to his rapidly increasing creative fertility; only much later, in Leipzig, was Bach to compose again for that instrument with such fervour. In Weimar, apart from consolidating all that he had learned so far, Bach also began to apply the principles of the Italian concerto to his own work, treating the theme in a decidedly modern way and even combining two themes in a way which foreshadows the techniques of the sonata. An instance of this is found in the *Toccata in C major*, BWV 564 which he probably composed in about 1709. It has three movements, toccata, adagio and fugue, thus absorbing the three-movement concerto form. The solo passages for the manuals and pedals are on a massive scale. Wide-ranging fantasy combines here with cadenza-like style in an uninhibited display of virtuosity:

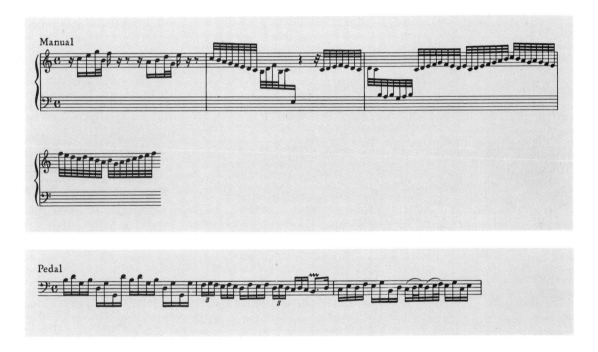

The adagio that follows is a slow concerto movement of a type that Bach was to return to in later years. Above a tutti comprising an ostinato bass leaping over wide intervals and richly harmonized middle voices, the solo line rises in an arching monologue:

This is an application of the new idea of a solo line with accompaniment that Bach was to use again in his Weimar cantatas. The movement does not end, however, on this note of unity, for Bach adds a section marked "grave" full of daring harmonies reminiscent of such great masters of the organ as Girolamo Frescobaldi.

Towards the end of his time in Weimar, probably in 1716, Bach wrote the *Fantasia and Fugue in C minor*, BWV 537. The fantasia contains two themes, of which the first

is immediately treated fugally, while the second is characterized by sighing quaver motifs which are taken up imitatively in other voices:

The two themes have an element of contrast between them. The fugue which follows contains three themes and is again very closely related to sonata form. These works demonstrate the new ideas permitting Bach's freely-composed organ works. He had taken the first major stride into a new domain. With the organ works written in Weimar Bach had become a master of his art.

The *Nekrolog* includes, in its authors' list of Bach's works: "Six Trios for organ with pedal obbligato". These are the six organ sonatas written, according to Forkel, for Wilhelm Friedemann Bach. They must have been composed between 1725 and 1729, that is, during the first years in Leipzig. In contrast to his chamber sonatas, all but one of the organ sonatas are in three movements. They rely in some respects on the technique of the trio sonata. All six works are written throughout on three separate staves, as is usual for the organ and in keeping with their essentially polyphonic construction. There is also a touch of modernity, however, in that both outer movements contain two themes which are manipulated in such a way that their treatment foreshadows the technique of formal development. The middle movements are characterized by expressive cantilena, yet counterpoint is by no means rejected. It is not only by comparison with the sonatas written in Cöthen that these works represent something new in Bach's work, but in the context of his organ music in general. They provide an exemplary extension of his art. Writing in 1774, nearly a quarter of a century after his father's death, Carl Philipp Emanuel recorded these revealing words to Johann Nikolaus Forkel: "The six clavier trios, which, because of their numbering form a set, are some of the best things that my dear departed father ever did. They still sound very well even now and give me such pleasure although they are over fifty years old. Some of the adagios could not, even today, be written in a more singing style."

While he was in Leipzig, Bach composed a marvellous series of preludes and fugues, those in B minor, C minor, E minor and E flat major (BWV 544, 546, 548, and 552),

works which also signalled the end of the golden era of German organ music. Here, Bach raises the form of the Prelude and Fugue to symphonic proportions. As far as we know, these pieces were not written on commission nor were they required in the line of duty. They are the spontaneous expression of his creative genius, the culmination of a lifetime's experience.

In the early part of the eighteenth century it was still not customary for any clear distinction to be made between music written for the organ and that intended for other keyboard instruments. While the place of the organ was necessarily in the church, the clavichord and harpsichord reigned in the home, the harpsichord being also widely used for chamber music and concerts. Of these two, the clavichord, with its weaker tone, was more suitable for domestic occasions, while the stronger voiced harpsichord (like the organ) was used as a continuo instrument in the church and in the opera house too: it was from the harpsichord that the Kapellmeister or Cantor would direct the performance.

Many of Bach's keyboard works are playable on both clavichord and harpsichord, but others require a two-manual harpsichord with the potential for changing registration. Bach also wrote pieces for harpsichord with pedals, and these works overlap to a certain extent with his organ music. All three instruments were generally designated "Clavier".

Bach's earliest extant keyboard pieces date from his time in Lüneburg, and it is possible that one keyboard fugue was even written in Ohrdruf. It is impossible to tell how much Bach was writing for the keyboard at this very early stage, but several works date from Arnstadt and are of interest both in relation to the composer's life and the historical development of the forms. Bach dedicated a Capriccio in E major (BWV 993) to his eldest brother with whom he was living in Ohrdruf: "In honour of Johann Christoph Bach". Another Capriccio, this time in B major (BWV 992), was written on the occasion of the departure of his brother Johann Jakob from Thuringia to serve at the Swedish court. It bears a descriptive subtitle: "On the departure of his beloved brother", and the six movements amusingly describe the sequence of events on this occasion:

1. Arioso: Coaxing by his friends to dissuade him from his journey.
2. A description of the various calamities which could befall him in foreign countries.
3. Adagiosissimo. A general lament of his friends.
4. All the friends, since they see that it cannot be otherwise, come and take leave of him.
5. Aria di Postiglione. (Postillion's Air).
6. Fuga all'imitatione di Posta. (Fugue in imitation of a post-horn.)

The immediate stimulus to the nineteen-year-old Bach to write to such a pictorial programme may have come from the six keyboard sonatas on Biblical studies that Kuhnau, then Cantor of St Thomas's, had published in Leipzig in 1700. But young Bach, with his Capriccio, had already leapt ahead of his much respected predecessor.

Most of Bach's early keyboard works belong to the Weimar years. They offer a clear indication of his growing mastery of the keyboard as a performer and a composer; they also served for teaching purposes, and this is always an important element in his keyboard music.

He wrote a number of keyboard fugues, some on themes of his own composition, some on themes taken from other composers, notably Italians. As we have already indicated, the keyboard works of the Weimar period reflect his interest in the Italian concerto. In all, he made sixteen transcriptions from Vivaldi, Benedetto Marcello, Prince Johann Ernst, and Telemann, and these reworkings of concertos were of great help in increasing his assurance when it came to employing the concerto style in his own works. That this was so is clear from the Prelude and Fugue in A minor BWV 894, to take just one example. This is thought to date from the end of Bach's Weimar period, and is one of the most impressive examples of Bach's successful introduction of the motivic interplay of the concerto into the form of the prelude and fugue:

Fugal elements are subordinate to the concerto style and the contrapuntal voices are hardly allowed to develop but are reduced to the role of accompaniment by the virtuoso decoration of the theme:

Bach himself was clearly aware of the strength of this concerto-like development, for he later reworked both the prelude and the fugue as the outer movements of the Concerto for Flute, Violin, and Harpsichord (BWV 1044) for performance at his Collegium Musicum in Leipzig.

The masterpieces of Bach's keyboard music in Weimar are the seven toccatas which in all probability he composed around 1709/10. They continue in the tradition of the seventeenth century, most of them having four movements: an introductory prelude is followed by a fugue then an adagio, then another fugue to conclude the piece. The music covers a wide range, from the powerfully energetic to the unashamedly carefree, while the slow movements anticipate the intellectual depth of later masterpieces. Extraordinary demands are constantly made upon the performer. The term "toccata" was later dropped for this kind of four-movement work, and Bach wrote nothing in this form either in Cöthen or Leipzig. These works are still rather improvisatory and have a quality of spontaneity which in Bach's later years would be supplemented by a firmer intellectual control and a greater degree of individuality. They are the work of the virtuoso performer, and it should be remembered that Bach, one of the last great exponents of a dying art, probably improvised many more toccatas than he committed to paper.

Viewed as a whole, Bach's keyboard music presents a harmonious blending of creative and didactic aims, and this duality became an essential feature from the Cöthen years onwards, extending into other areas of his work. (For a discussion of Bach as teacher and of the collections of keyboard works which he intended to be used for instruction, see Chapter 9.) Apart from the strong teaching tradition within his family, Bach's own experience in Weimar and his duties in Cöthen all inclined him towards the production of music specifically for teaching purposes. He wrote the *Clavier-Büchlein for Wilhelm Friedemann Bach* for his eldest son, dating the title page January 1720. Two years later he composed the first of the *Notebooks for Anna Magdalena* and also Part I of the *Well Tempered Clavier* (both dated 1722) and these were followed, one year later, by the Inventions.

It was probably in Cöthen that Bach really occupied himself with the genre of the suite, though there is no doubt that he had been acquainted with the dance form associated with it for a long time. Two series of harpsichord suites were written in Cöthen, the six *French Suites* and the six *English Suites*. (In neither case was the national designation given by Bach himself.) Five of the *French Suites* come from the *Notebook for Anna Magdalena* and Bach called them "Suite pour le Clavessin". Each is based on the sequence of Allemande — Courante — Sarabande — Gigue, extended to six, seven or eight movements by the insertion of extra movements such as Air, Menuet, Gavotte, Polonaise, Bourrée and Loure after the Sarabande. Although the basic shape of each dance type is retained, Bach was able to stylize it most ingeniously, and, while limiting himself essentially to three-part writing and in some cases to transparent two-part writing, he nevertheless presents the performer with many problems. The freedom and command displayed by Bach in these suites places them at the apogee of this form:

Bach succeeds admirably in preserving the essential character of each dance in the suites while presenting it with the greatest variety; yet he never oversteps the limits of domestic music-making. The *English Suites* are more concerto-like in their form and brilliance. Each opens with a prelude of considerable proportions. Officially, the prelude is not an integral part of the suite, thus from the start the piece has less of the suite about it and more of the concerto. The fact that Bach repeated this device in each of the six suites would suggest a deliberate effort on his part to extend and strengthen the form, to take it beyond its traditional limits. This was characteristic of Bach and clearly important to his way of thinking. In the *English Suites* the dance movements conform more consistently to the traditional models than in the *French Suites*. The preludes are the most characteristic movements, for they are only conceivable in terms of the harpsichord.

Each suite consists of the four usual dances with additional ones bringing the number of movements up to six or seven.

Apparently it was while Bach was in Cöthen that he also wrote the first version of a work which has, ever since, excited a special degree of admiration: the *Chromatic Fantasia and Fugue*, BWV 903. Like so many of Bach's works, the original manuscript is lost and we only have copies in many different versions. It was changed and extended in Leipzig and reached the final form, the one in which we now know it, in 1730. In his biography of Bach, Forkel was enthusiastic about it: "This Fantasia," he wrote, "is unique and remains without equal." Bach had already written numerous fantasias and fugues whose novelty and unprecedented technical demands were an expression of his constant striving to progress as an artist. This work is artistically, structurally, and technically daring, boundlessly imaginative in the fantasia, yet highly disciplined in the fugue, so that the latter may even seem at odds with the extravagance that has preceded it. The essence of the fantasia is improvisation; eschewing traditional forms, its expression of subjective emotions and display of technical keyboard brilliance seems to know no bounds. It is introduced by a daring run:

The flow of melody, of arpeggios and of harmonic tensions that had only been made possible by equal temperament, is only stemmed by the introduction of an instrumental recitative:

In the fugue chromaticism becomes immediately evident in the melodic shape of the theme:

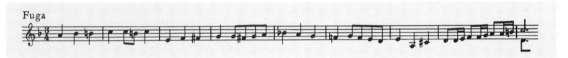

But this chromaticism in turn also gives rise to wide-ranging harmonies, penetrating into distant and unexpected regions. He uses the fugue almost as an imaginative framework within which the daring of the fantasia is continued and its ideas developed along new lines in a concerto-like style of dialogue. This work points the way towards the *Well Tempered Clavier*, with its tonal comprehensiveness and virtually unprecedented variety of mood evoked by both melody and harmony. The *Chromatic Fantasia and Fugue* is, in the last analysis, an overwhelming, individual and unique work, of breathtaking greatness. At the same time, it is part of a whole into which even this work which defies categorization can be happily integrated and assimilated.

76. German Clavichord, second quarter of the 18th century.

This judgement is strengthened by the keyboard works which date from the Leipzig period. To begin with, Bach's move to the Thomasschule had brought quite a different area of activity into prominence, that of the cantata. But teaching was an important part of his duties in Leipzig; he had to prove that he was not only an experienced Kapellmeister but a composer who knew how to write for the keyboard and was fully equal to his duties.

From 1726 onwards Bach began to publish his keyboard partitas himself, first individually and then, in 1731, collected in one volume as *Clavier-Übung I*. Two of the pieces dated from 1725 and had been included in the second *Notebook for Anna Magdalena*. This set a precedent for several collections of keyboard music which, over the next twenty years, themselves rounded off his lifetime's work in this sphere. Remembering the collections of his keyboard works that Bach made earlier in Cöthen, we see that this was not only a characteristic of his last years. We shall return to this later. Moreover, there was nothing new in the publishing of such collections in particular forms. For instance, Kuhnau had published his own *Clavierübung*, so Bach was following a local tradition apart from all the more far-reaching implications. The title page of Bach's collection reads:

Clavier-Übung

consisting in

Preludes, Allemandes, Courantes,

Sarabandes, Gigues, Minuets

and other galanteries

composed for the delight of amateurs

by

Johann Sebastian Bach

present Capellmeister to His Highness the Prince of Anhalt-Cöthen

and

Director Chori Musici Lipsiensis

OPUS I

Part I

Published by the Author

1731

The mention of particular forms in order to arouse the interest of keyboard players was evidently of more importance to Bach than the fact that these were partitas. These six works, with their multi-movement structure, show several new features. As in the *English Suites*, there is an introductory movement, but here Bach selects six different forms, some old, some new, with which to commence the works: prelude (or "preambulum"), sinfonia, fantasia, overture, and toccata. And besides the specific dance movements usually found in the suite, he includes forms with little or no connection with the dance, such as scherzo, burlesque or capriccio. Thus these six partitas represent a truly practical "manual" for the keyboard suite which is not only a compendium of Bach's own experience but draws upon the whole tradition of this musical form.

That Bach's intentions with regard to his *Clavier-Übung* went further, is made plain by his designating the first collection "Part I". Further parts were obviously intended to follow, and they did; in 1735 Part II appeared, with this title page:

Second Part
of the
Clavier-Übung
consisting of
a Concerto after the Italian taste
and
an Overture in the French style
for a
Harpsichord with two manuals
composed for the delight and edification of music-lovers
by
Johann Sebastian Bach
Capellmeister to His Highness the Prince of Saxe-Weissenfels
and
Director Chori Musici Lipsiensis . . .

This breaks new ground in keyboard music: Bach was moving into new forms and new styles. He was also proving his mastery of all forms and demonstrating that there was nothing that the keyboard player could not learn from him. Already familiar with both the concerto and the overture, he now presented them in solo keyboard works. How could a "Clavier-Übung" exist without a concerto? Bach had examined it and used its characteristic elements a hundred times. Now the three-movement structure was transferred to the keyboard, the typical interchange between soloist and tutti being imitated by changes of manual and registration on the harpsichord. Tutti and solo passages were also indicated by their own themes, itself evidence of a capacity for motivic interweaving. This led almost inevitably to the principle of thematic development which was becoming ever more prominent in the sonata. Thus the *Italian Concerto*, without ceding the basic principles of the concerto for an instant even though it features a solo harpsichord *without* an orchestra, can also be seen as opening the way to the concept of the sonata. Yet again Bach was extending a form beyond its natural limits. The themes of the first movement are:

The second movement is an andante. One of the most beautiful slow movements that Bach ever wrote, it is also remarkable for his complete notation of the ornamental decoration to the melodic line, by which it becomes an illuminating document of performance practice. Over an ostinato figure:

arches a melody that is an inimitable blend of energy and lyricism, inner strength and calm grandeur:

The musical language of this cantabile solo comes close to that of many vocal arias. By contrast, the last movement, presto, is a spirited and jolly finale that takes its cue from the syncopation at the beginning of the theme and continues with brilliant passage-work. The essence of the concerto finds its culmination here in boisterous virtuosity:

77. Harpsichord, attributed to Johann Heinrich Harrass, Grossbreitenbach, Thuringia, 1712.

The *French Overture* in B minor (BWV 831) has certain affinities with Bach's orchestral suites which were indebted to French models, but the number of movements is extended to eleven: Overture — Courante — Gavotte I and II – Passepied I and II — Sarabande – Bourrée I and II — Gigue — Echo. All the conceivable possibilities seem to have been brought together here. An Echo is added to the Gigue, which was traditionally the final movement: it is a delicate musical reflection with no dance-like features.

On 30 September 1739 the following announcement appeared in the *Leipziger Zeitungen*: "Enthusiasts of Mr Bach's Clavier-Übung are cordially informed that the third part is now completed and is available from the Author in Leipzig, price 3 thalers." The publication coincided with the Michaelmas fair, and followed Part II by just four years. Part III contains the Four Duets already mentioned. They are again reminiscent of the Inventions written in Cöthen, but in their scope and their artistic character they go well beyond the earlier compositions. These pieces also express a paradigmatic intention on the part of their composer. The duet principle is displayed four times, but each time the mood is different. In the first duet the basic tone is that of a fantasia, featuring chromatic motifs, undercutting the severity of two-part imitation by an impression of improvisatorial extravagance and thus evoking a tension between the formal principle and emotional expression:

The second duet is characterized more by composure, a sense of energy and of logical development. This is expressed in the diatonic clarity of the theme and is supported by the ingenious symmetry of the internal structure as the duet develops:

How different from the amiability and charm of the third duet, whose rocking semiquaver figures seem weightless and light-hearted:

In 1742, after only three years, Bach published Part IV of the *Clavier-Übung*:

Clavier-Übung
consisting in an
ARIA
with several variations
for Harpsichord with 2 manuals
composed for the edification
and delight of music-lovers by
Johann Sebastian Bach . . .

With the art of the variation Bach was returning to a form that he had neglected for a long time, aside from the necessary presence of variation as a part of any musical form. It was logical that the variation form as such should claim a place within his *Clavier-Übung*, as much for the sake of the composer as for the player.

The structure of this cycle; known as the *Goldberg Variations*, is marked by Bach's spacious and well-ordered musical thought. The theme is an aria of thirty-two bars:

It occurs not only at the beginning, but also at the end, where it rounds off the thirty variations and summarizes them. The number of movements is thus raised to thirty-two. The variation theme is modelled on the bass line of the aria:

The sequence of variations demonstrates Bach's ability to exploit the theme without ever abandoning it. Diversity and method are combined. Variations in canon are used in numbers one to nine:

variations with brilliant figuration:

78. *The Well Tempered Clavier, Bk. 1, No.15, three-part fugue in G major, BWV 860, autograph.*

and free variations of the most diverse character:

Variation 16 is a formal Overture, divided into two sections by a pause. Both player and listener are made aware of the composer's profoundly expressive arrangement.

The cycle did not exhaust Bach's imagination in this form, but the set is unprecedented in its comprehensiveness and provides an encyclopedia of the art of keyboard variations. It did not, even so, mark the end of Bach's collections of keyboard music.

In 1744 he finished the second *Well Tempered Clavier*. The idea behind the collection, that of demonstrating the opportunities afforded by equal temperament, had been fully realized in the first collection. Strictly speaking, the second was superfluous. So why did he do it? There were probably sound artistic reasons; he possibly felt that there were greater depths to be plumbed by a repetition of the exercise; it may have been a further expression of his need to collect individual Preludes and Fugues, make final versions of them, and present them in a predetermined sequence; he may even have seen it as an extension of the *Clavier-Übung*. The instinct to plan and to organize his work remained throughout Bach's life.

Bach finished the *Well Tempered Clavier II* six years before his death. Not only had he been the most outstanding keyboard performer of the first half of the eighteenth century, but he had raised the art of keyboard composition to a level of unprecedented importance in the history of music. From now on his works were to provide a yardstick for all keyboard music, and to serve as an example for every great keyboard composer in the generations to come.

79. *Leipzig – Zimmermann's coffee-house, No.14 Katharinenstrasse, destroyed in World War II.*

Concertos and Overtures

The relatively modern concept of the instrumental concerto emerged at the end of the seventeenth century as a result of that development of instrumental music that found its culmination in the achievements of Vivaldi. During this same period Johann Sebastian Bach was making his own analysis of the concerto in Weimar and finding in it elements that suited his needs. The fluid dialogue between soloist (or soloists) and orchestra, the unprecedented motivic development, the extension of the solo parts by means of variation, the new flexibility and elegance of the instrumental writing which effortlessly incorporated passages of extreme technical difficulty and, in the aria-like slow movements, passages of an almost vocal cantabile that permitted a hitherto unheard-of expressiveness — all these achievements were in accordance with the growing refinement of the composer's sensibilities and with his musical experience and reflected his intellectual and emotional development. Between the simultaneous development of the concerto and "dramma per musica" there exists a necessary connection. The prominence afforded to the solo singer in opera as an individual acting in relation to the accompanying instruments was in many respects similar to the position of the soloist in the concerto. And there is another aspect worth considering: was the juxtaposition of solo and tutti, of the prima donna and the accompanying ensemble not in some way a reflection of social conditions? Was not life itself in those times based on the juxtaposition of the elevated individual possessing power and wealth with the masses subject to him? It is surely not far-fetched to see the concerto, for all the undeniable autonomy of music, translating the world into musical terms.

For Bach, as for most of his contemporaries, concerto-style writing, with its organized interplay of solo and tutti, became a most important principle of musical composition. He used it in two different ways: first as an instrument form (in the solo concerto and concerto grosso); and second as a principle of performance which could be used in many other forms, both instrumental and vocal. It is the instrumental form with which we are at present concerned. Bach devoted himself to this form both in Cöthen and Leipzig, where, as Kapellmeister, he had orchestras at his disposal for which he was expected to compose suitable music. It was in Weimar, however, that he began to make the concerto form his own. Whether, while in Weimar, he wrote concertos with orchestral accompaniment which have been lost, cannot be ascertained. It is, however, certain that the instrumental concerto was in the repertoire of the court orchestra in Cöthen, and, as Kapellmeister, it was Bach's responsibility to renew and enlarge this repertoire. Unfortunately we have no catalogue of the music in the possession of the court and only a limited knowledge of the performed repertoire. Of Bach's own Cöthen compositions by

no means all are still extant, and the number that we have could yet be reduced by the discovery that many of the works attributed to the Cöthen period may indeed have originated in Leipzig. This is true for the concertos *inter alia*. On the other hand, it is very likely that Bach used concertos composed in Cöthen as the basis for cantatas written in Leipzig. In any event, although we have no complete picture of the concertos he wrote in Cöthen, we possess enough of them to form a good idea of the way in which Bach's concerto writing developed and of how the earlier works paved the way for the later ones.

Pride of place must, of course, go to the six works which Philipp Spitta labelled the *Brandenburg Concertos*. Dedicated to the Margrave Christian Ludwig of Brandenburg on 24 March 1721, they were not written on a commission but belonged, for the most part, to Bach's Cöthen repertoire and were simply placed at the Margrave's disposal by means of the dedication. Their scoring is within the capacities of just such a well-equipped court orchestra as Bach would have had during the first years in Cöthen, where any deficiencies could have been redressed by calling on musicians from neighbouring court orchestras when the need arose. We can safely assume that the concertos were never intended to form a cycle, for each is totally individual and self-contained. As always, Bach shows an admirable versatility in the structure, the scoring, the melodic invention and the expressive character of these works. Different combinations of soloists are used in each concerto. Two of the works do not fit into the standard three-movement scheme: No. 1 (BWV 1046), whose extended sequence of five movements with two additional trios is reminiscent of the suite, and No. 3 (BWV 1048), where we find, in place of a fully written-out third movement, only two chords marked *adagio* which were probably intended to be expanded into a movement proper by improvisation on a solo instrument. In No. 5 (BWV 1050) three solo instruments are used: flute, violin and harpsichord, but by giving the harpsichord an extended virtuoso cadenza in the first movement, Bach gives a prominence to this instrument that foreshadows the harpsichord concerto, a form previously unknown.

In all six concertos the first movements are extensive, yet, typically, they lose nothing

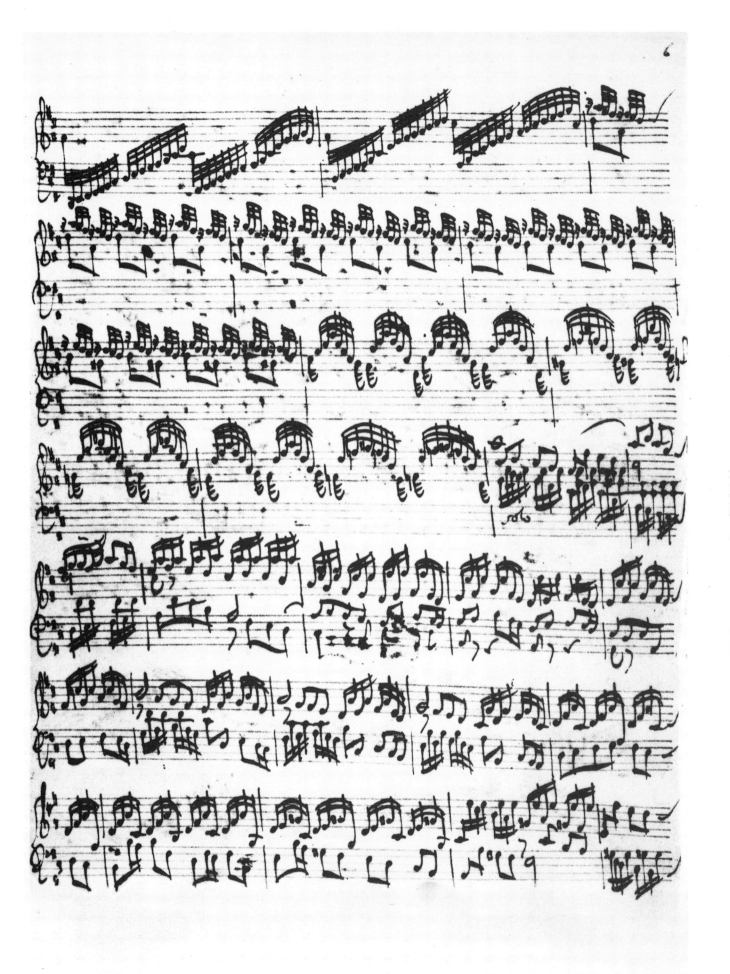

81. *Brandenburg Concerto No.5 in D major, BWV 1050, extract from the harpsichord cadenza in the first movement, autograph.*

in concentration. Their predominantly tripartite structure foreshadows classical sonata form and in the interplay between soloists and tutti, based on the material stated in the tutti ritornello, we find a hint of the treatment of themes and motives which was to play a fundamental role in the classical Viennese style.

The themes in the Brandenburg Concertos are among the most perfectly finished to be found in any concertos from the first half of the eighteenth century. The slow movements are dominated by the soloists, the orchestral accompaniment sometimes being omitted altogether and only the continuo group retained. The themes unfold with expressive individuality, and as they develop, usually through imitation, have a sense of measured order:

The final movements show a preference for a cheerful, dance-like style primarily determined by the nature of the theme and developed with a joyous energy, even virtuosity. Both because of the limited forces of a court orchestra in central Germany in the early eighteenth century, and because of the individuality of the writing, these works cannot be considered as Italianate concerti grossi. The larger orchestra employed by the Italian composers would certainly not have lent itself to the subtle interplay of solo and tutti that Bach achieves with an ensemble that seldom numbered more than eighteen and was sometimes (for instance in No. 6) required to be considerably smaller than that. These concertos are poised, so to speak, on the dividing line between chamber and orchestral music. They summarize all the experience and potentialities available to a composer like Bach around the year 1720 and together with Handel's Grand Concertos, Op. 6, represent the highest peak of the Baroque concerto.

We come now to the concertos for violin and harpsichord, some of which are for a single soloist, others for two or more. These clearly belonged to the repertoire of the Leipzig Collegium Musicum and were composed while Bach was its director. The harpsichord concertos for a single solo instrument are all transcriptions of concertos originally written by Bach for other instruments, mainly for violin. The Concerto in A minor for four harpsichords and string orchestra is, however, based on Vivaldi's Concerto in B minor (Op. 10 no. 3) for four violins. In recent years some of Bach's solo concertos have been reconstructed from his own re-workings, the original versions having been lost. All of them employ the three-movement form of the Italian concerto. In all we have more than thirty concertos for various instrumentations in original or reconstructed versions that Bach wrote in Cöthen or Leipzig. What he may have written earlier in Weimar is not known.

Among the solo concertos the Violin Concertos in A minor (BWV 1041) and E major (BWV 1042) have achieved a considerable popularity, as has also, to an even greater extent, the Double Concerto for Two Violins in D minor (BWV 1043). These too set up a thrilling tension between soloist(s) and orchestra despite a strong link between the orchestral ritornellos and solo episodes:

Bach does not restrict himself, however, to employing the same techniques over and over again; he finds different solutions and retains a clear thematic or motivic distinction between solo and tutti:

Concerto a Cembalo obligato Con Stromenti

I.R.Schellenberg delin.

I.R.Holzhalb sculps.

82. *Keyboard concerto played by the Zurich "Gesellschaft auf dem Musiksaal" (Music room Society), 1777.*

One of the most beautiful examples of the art of the concerto in Bach's hands is another work which would have been in the repertoire of the Collegium Musicum and was first performed at Zimmermann's coffee-house (or garden). This is the A minor Concerto for flute, violin, harpsichord, and string orchestra (BWV 1044) known as the Triple Concerto. Here Bach has again re-worked his own material. The outer movements are based on the Prelude and Fugue in A minor (BWV 894) written in Weimar, and the slow middle movement is probably based on a trio, yet to be discovered, which Bach also utilized for the middle movement of the Organ Sonata in D minor (BWV 527). In the Triple Concerto the older models are endowed with a new artistic quality. In recasting his own works Bach showed no less mastery than in his re-working of pieces by other composers. Such re-working was still a matter of course in the early eighteenth century. It is particularly impressive to see how Bach seizes the opportunities afforded by the three soloists to enlarge the concept of the concerto, especially in the way he combines motivic and thematic transformation with the concerto-style interplay of forces. A comparison of BWV 894 with BWV 1044 makes the distinction clear:

In the *Adagio ma non tanto e dolce*, Bach, by dispensing with the accompanying orchestra, gives the movement the feeling of chamber music. It is a quartet for flute, violin and the two obbligato harpsichord parts. This concerto is splendid proof that the re-working of his own or other composers' pieces was by no means a mechanical process for Bach, nor merely a matter of professional craftsmanship. In many cases the older model served simply as a stimulus to the imagination, to be used or discarded in the process of fashioning a genuinely new work. Each of his re-workings is thus a kind of resumption or continuation of the process of composition, taking a different set of circumstances into account and applying a different approach. This is entirely congruent with Bach's ideas about music.

An examination of the concertos themselves is not enough to allow for a full appreciation of Bach's creative relationship with the concerto style as a principle of composition, for there was probably not a single form that he used into which he did not work elements of this technique. This can be seen in the field of chamber music and, in an equal degree, in vocal forms too. The practice finds its counterpart in Bach's integration of other forms such as the fugue and aria into his concertos. He is certainly not the only composer to do this, but the practice is particularly pronounced in the works of Bach.

This refusal to be bound by the formal characteristics of any genre, but to adapt them freely and imaginatively, is also to be seen in Bach's orchestral overtures. Four of these survive, in the form of the German Orchestral Suite: the Overtures in C major (BWV 1066), B minor (BWV 1067), and two in D major (BWV 1068 and 1069). The designation "overture" first appeared as a movement in the form of a French overture which introduced a suite. The oldest form with many movements in German orchestral music, the suite was widespread in seventeenth-century Germany and was subject to elaborate treatment. Important contributions to the form had been made by Johann Rosenmüller, Johann Joseph Fux and Philipp Krieger, and it was also an important form for Bach's contemporaries Telemann and Handel. It is not clear when Bach wrote his first orchestral overture, but there is no doubt that the four extant works are the survivors of what must have been a considerably larger group of compositions dating from his years in Cöthen and Leipzig. They are ceremonial works, as we can see from the rhetorical gestures of the opening movements and also from the scoring. This style is in keeping with the original function of the French overture at court, where it served as introductory music for performances of ballet. In Bach's time it had come to express a distinctly bourgeois feeling of elation: the courtly function had been adapted to bourgeois use.

The Overture in B minor (BWV 1067) for flute and string orchestra is of special interest in that it fuses the orchestral suite and the concerto. Leaving intact the sequence of dance movements — to which the overture provides a festive prelude — Bach enriches the whole by the introduction of a solo flute that he provides with a concerto-like part, which gives the whole work a distinctly concerto-like feel. There are long passages in which the flute and the first violins play in unison:

and the flute is only given prominence in a few solo episodes, the most important of which is the *double* of the polonaise:

83. Students making music.

and the final *badinerie*, where the jollity of the dance and the virtuosity of the concerto combine:

In both the D major Overtures (BWV 1068 and 1069) Bach employs three trumpets and timpani as well as oboes, bassoon, strings and continuo. For the period, and taking into consideration the specific conditions under which Bach was working, this was opulent scoring; it would, for instance, have been beyond the means of a small court orchestra. All four works survive in copies only, and this makes it more difficult than ever to determine when they were composed. After Bach and his contemporaries the German orchestral suite developed no further. Bach's works in the genre, infused as they are with elements of the concerto, point towards the paths which were to become the most important in the future development of orchestral music.

84. *Concerto in C minor for two harpsichords and string orchestra, BWV 1062, and Sonata in A major for flute and harpsichord, BWV 1032, first page of the autograph.*

85. *Leipzig – St Thomas's Church, interior with organ gallery and choir gallery.*

The Cantatas

In one area of Bach's activity, the cantata, we find his whole world embraced in words and music. Not only did they occupy him from as early as 1707, but they exist in an inexhaustible abundance and variety. Yet it is a strange fact that, while our knowledge of the music of Bach has become ever more profound and performances of it ever more frequent over the last one hundred years or more, the cantatas remain among his least explored compositions. In various forms, writing cantatas was a part of Bach's professional duties throughout his life. The earliest extant examples that we have were written in Mühlhausen, for the church. In Cöthen the emphasis was on secular cantatas for the court. In Leipzig, the cantorate allowed him to return to the church cantata and to develop and enrich the form in a quite unprecedented way, while simultaneously adding to the number of secular cantatas he wrote for both court and town. The heights that he eventually reached were never again attained by any other composer.

The cantata originated in Italy, its style having developed from the early opera and from the oratorio. It was adopted in Germany in the seventeenth century and soon became a mainstay of the more elaborate music of the Protestant church as a vehicle for the telling of stories from the Bible. Until about 1700 the texts were taken exclusively from the Bible or chorale verses, but a new page in the history of the cantata was turned when Pastor Erdmann Neumeister began writing librettos specifically for the cantatas to be sung in the Weissenfels court chapel which was under the direction of Philipp Krieger. Neumeister's texts, which were always linked to a particular Sunday or feast-day in the church calendar, soon achieved great popularity and from 1704 appeared collected in booklets entitled Sacred Cantatas and Sacred Concertos respectively. In one of his prefaces the author explained: "Briefly, a cantata bears a closer resemblance to an excerpt from an opera than to anything else, comprising recitatives and arias." Philipp Heinrich Erlebach, Georg Philipp Telemann, and Johann Sebastian Bach all set texts by Pastor Neumeister, who was soon serving as a model to numerous other poets.

As was to be expected, the new style of cantata text was not welcomed throughout the Protestant Church, however, for while the orthodox Lutherans accepted them willingly the Pietists regarded any suggestion of operatic style detrimental to the purity of the faith. Their opposition did not hinder the development of the cantata, however. The new texts were, of course, still based upon the Scriptures, but treated with an individuality that called for a correspondingly expressive musical setting. The possibilities offered by the interplay of choruses, arias, and recitatives were virtually inexhaustible and allowed full scope to the subjectivity so germane to the growing self-awareness of the times in which they were written; yet their devotion to their subject-matter was never in doubt.

Until he went to Weimar in 1712, Bach's only cantatas were those that he composed following the older German models he had known since his childhood in Thuringia, in Lüneburg and when he was with Buxtehude in Lübeck in 1705–6. "Cantata" is in fact anachronistic at this stage, for many decades were still to pass before the term became current in church music, the earlier designations being *Motetto*, *Kirchenstück*, *Dialogus* or *Concerto*. In the early "cantatas", the tradition of the German motet is indeed still clear in the dependence upon biblical texts or chorales which were only minimally complemented by poetic material; yet Bach, at the age of twenty-two, already displays an astonishing maturity. With the cantata written in Mühlhausen, probably in 1707, *Gottes Zeit ist die allerbeste Zeit* (BWV 106), his superiority to all other German composers of cantatas was established once and for all. This cantata is an *actus tragicus*, or cantata of mourning. What event prompted it is unknown. Bach's scoring is in keeping with the theme of mourning; he uses only the softer-toned instruments: two recorders, two viole da gamba and continuo. The solo voices are alto, tenor, and bass, and there is a four-part chorus. The scale of the work may place it within the intimate context of chamber music, yet it is many-layered, expressive and well crafted. The opening "sonatina" is reflective and sensitive. The art of the old German motet (in the chorus "Gottes Zeit") and of the sacred concerto (in the alto solo "In deine Hände") are manifest in the composition which combines chorus and solo with an instrumental chorale quotation in the central movement ("Es ist der alte Bund"); the interweaving of so many strands is typical of Bach:

116

Many cantatas of an even earlier date have undoubtedly been lost, but we can see from the *actus tragicus* how Bach was already welding words and music into an artistic whole. The work summarizes his early experience of the form, and from this point we can see that the step forward to the Neumeister type of cantata was clearly indicated.

Bach took this step in Weimar, certainly no later than 1714. His preparation for it began a year earlier with his first secular cantata, *Was mir behagt, ist nur die muntre Jagd*, the "Hunting Cantata". This was undoubtedly written at the request of Weimar's Duke Wilhelm Ernst for the splendid celebrations of the birthday of Duke Christian of Saxe-Weissenfels, who was rather fond of flamboyant display. It was performed on 21 February 1713. Bach's appointment as Konzertmeister a year later provided him with a direct incentive to write church cantatas, for he was obliged to provide one every month and directed the performances himself. Before he left Weimar he had already, therefore, written numerous cantatas to texts of the Neumeister type, twenty-one of which are still

in existence. Bach's evident intention was to write a whole cycle of cantatas based upon the church calendar, but his departure for Cöthen intervened. His first cantata upon a text by Neumeister was *Gleichwie der Regen und Schnee vom Himmel fällt* (BWV 18).

Bach's most important literary collaborator in Weimar was the court poet and leader of the Consistory, Salomo Franck, who, possibly as the result of encouragement from Bach, began writing texts for cantatas in 1715, modelling himself on Neumeister. He wrote sacred and secular texts for the court in Weimar, and in these the use of arias and recitatives was also customary. The influence of Neumeister showed itself in two kinds of texts, both of which Bach was setting in Weimar. The first was a sequence of recitatives and arias which did not draw at all upon the words of the Bible or chorale verses. The second combined recitatives and arias with scriptural texts and/or chorale verses. More than half of the extant cantatas of Bach are of the second type, and in these Bach took the most important step in the development of the cantata, a step which had profound musical consequences. Here, Bach endowed the cantata with a richness of expression the like of which had never before been heard. At the same time, by his introduction of chorales and elaborately worked choral movements in the tradition of vocal polyphony, Bach made the cantata into a form that could integrate different elements to an astonishing degree. The transition to texts of the Neumeister type was the base upon which all Bach's future cantata-writing was to be built. Weimar was therefore no mere "preparation" for later achievements. It was here that he mastered the craft of writing the cantata.

In August 1714 Bach directed the first performance of his solo cantata *Mein Herze schwimmt im Blut* (BWV 199). Its text, by Georg Christian Lehms, expressed the idea of man as sinner finding consolation in the sacrifice of Christ. Bach's music is exceptionally vivid. The succession of recitatives and arias adopts a modern, dramatic form and the melodies are deeply expressive.

Bach here shows his readiness to break with tradition by inserting a completely unexpected recitative at the end of the middle section of the aria before the reprise.

In Cöthen Bach produced fewer cantatas than he had in Weimar. It was only when the requirements of his post in Leipzig demanded cantata composition that he began once more to pour his energies into this kind of work. In 1723 he had reached that stage of his creative development at which it was appropriate that the cantata should become the most important part of his output, and it remained so for a great many years. He was required, as cantor, to prepare a cantata for every Sunday and every feast-day throughout the year, and saw it as a matter of professional pride that he should prove himself equal to writing his own for these occasions. However, no elaborate music was performed during Lent, which lasted about eight weeks, nor when there was a period of local mourning.

Rehearsal time was limited. He had to depend upon the skill of the best pupils from the Thomasschule and on former students now at the university, on the four *Stadtpfeifer* (wind instrument players employed by the town council), three *Kunstgeiger* (string players of a rather more sophisticated kind) and the student members of the Collegium Musicum. During performances he had to employ all his own experience and confidence. His demanding scores are themselves a proof of the ability of his singers and instrumentalists, however, for it would hardly be doing justice either to his integrity or to his working procedures to assume that he would write pieces that were beyond the capabilities of the performers and bound to result in disasters. All the same, one should not assume either that the same standard of performance was expected in the early eighteenth century as we expect today.

It was part of the tradition of church music that, at the end of the year, the cantatas that had been composed throughout the preceding twelve months should be collected into a single compilation. Each annual compilation would therefore comprise all the cantatas necessary for every Sunday and every feast-day of the church year. With the inclusion of the cantatas written earlier and subsequently performed (sometimes in altered versions) in Leipzig, Bach could have achieved five such compilations by the early 1730s, according to the *Nekrolog*. However, only three of them include the requisite number of works for a full cycle, while numbers four and five have considerable gaps.[9] We must assume that a considerable number of works were lost, and no claim of completeness can be made even for those that have survived. When Bach collected his first annual set of cantatas, he did not number them according to the church year but began with the date on which he assumed the Leipzig cantorate, which was the First Sunday after Trinity

(30 May) 1723. He compiled no less than fifty-six cantatas, whose manner of composition clearly indicates that he had exceptional choral and instrumental forces at his disposal, that he was a past master at the art of relating words and music and that he took local conditions into consideration. As a rule the cantatas open with a full-scale choral movement. This holds true of the very first cantata that Bach wrote in Leipzig: *Die Elenden sollen essen* (BWV 75). It is in two parts, one of which would have been sung before the sermon and one after, thus adding to the musical content of the service in a particularly profound way. In the opening movement the orchestra (strings, two oboes and continuo) combines with the four-part choir in the presentation of the text of the Psalm. The bipartite form of the movement respects the emotions inherent in the text and provides the musical equivalent of a profession of faith. A sense of gravity, of solemnity, is achieved by the contrast of rhythmically accentuated motives in the orchestra with a flowing cantabile line in the choral part. This is followed by a fugal setting of the concluding lines "Euer Herz soll ewig leben". The formality of this structure is reminiscent of the prelude and fugue combination which Bach used so often in his organ works.

Opening movements on this scale are also found in many other musical genres both vocal and instrumental such as the French Overture, concerto movements and the chorale prelude. Another technique that he uses here and was to use again frequently is that of the interpolated chorus, that is, of alternating choral sections with repeated instrumental ones and blending the whole into a single entity. Opening movements of the same kind are also to be found in Bach's next annual compilation of cantatas from the 1724/25 set. Here, perhaps through adherence to an old Leipzig tradition, Bach turned to the chorale cantata. This takes as its starting point the chorale appropriate for a certain Sunday (and therefore correlated with the text of the sermon), each verse of which provided the base for a cantata movement. By its dependence upon the chorale, the cantata acquired a particularly marked inner unity. The chorale texts were, moreover, not used as they stood, but were altered to a greater or lesser degree and the number of their verses curtailed to accord with the number of movements required. This allowed the relationship with the Gospel texts to be made clearer and also emphasized the variety of the movements. The first and last verse of the chorale however, were never altered. As in the chorale prelude, the opening movement usually presents the chorale melody with extensive elaboration. By contrast the last movement concentrates on the last verse of the chorale in a way designed to conclude the piece on a note of affirmation, with a four-part setting and the instruments doubling the voices (*colla parte*).

In November 1724 Bach composed the chorale cantata *Ach wie flüchtig, ach wie nichtig* (BWV 26). It is based on the chorale melody of the same name written in 1652 by Michael Franck. The thirteen verses of the original have been reduced to six and verses two to five have been re-written by an unknown hand. The chorale melody is as follows:

The opening movement presents the chorale line by line in an animated texture, characterized by rapid scales for the whole orchestra or for concertante groups of instruments.

What else could this possibly be than the "fickle" and "futile" ("flüchtig" and "nichtig") elements of life evoked in the title? The musical evocation is underlined by interjections from the altos, tenors and basses of the chorus and reaches a climax when the chorale is quoted by the soprano and horn. The musical image is complex and many-faceted and the structure is on three levels, yet the forthright statement of the chorale is completely unambiguous and conveys the universality of human experience.

The chorale cantatas in the 1724/25 set are also based on texts which have been adapted by an unknown hand. The last in this set is that written for Easter. For the remaining, missing, weeks of the year, Bach composed cantatas of the same type that he had been writing the previous year. Several are settings of texts written by the Leipzig poetess Christiane Marianne von Ziegler. By 1735 Bach had written nine more independent chorale cantatas which all share one special feature in that they are based on the original versions of the chorale texts. Although they were written over many years, Bach subsequently included them in the set for 1724/25.

By the time we come to the third of the annual sets, the picture of uninterrupted, concentrated cantata composition is already beginning to change. The pieces were not being written in such close succession nor do they evince such unity of style. Some of the poets were known in the Weimar period. We find here many cantatas of the dialogue type, one example of which is the Christmas cantata *Selig ist der Mann* (BWV 57), which is specifically designated a "Concerto in dialogo". The dialogue is between Jesus and the human soul, and Bach puts his own highly personal stamp upon it. As he had done in his first year in Leipzig, Bach entrusted the part of Jesus to a bass. The part of the soul aspiring to God was given to a soprano.

This set also includes a large number of cantatas in which Bach has taken over movements from previous instrumental works (overtures, concertos, solo partitas) and incorporated them sometimes unaltered, sometimes with changed instrumentation, sometimes with the addition of vocal parts.

There are no further annual sets or cycles which can be described as complete. Instead, individual works predominate from the end of the 1720s. So many works have been lost that it may never be possible to reconstruct a complete picture. The so-called Picander cycle may be an exception. Picander, whose real name was Christian Friedrich Henrici, published a set of original cantata texts in Leipzig in 1728 entitled: "Cantatas for Sundays and Feast Days throughout the year". In the foreword, dated 28 June 1728, he expresses his hope that there may be a possibility or even a likelihood of his pieces being set by Bach "so that maybe the inadequacy of their poetic grace could be compensated by the amiability of the incomparable Capellmeister Herr Bach, and these songs performed in the principal churches of the Godfearing town of Leipzig". Did Bach in the event live up to Picander's expectations? The question must remain forever unanswered, for despite the fact that Picander's texts for Bach were more numerous than those of any other poet, the works are all lost and we now have only six cantatas which might or might not have been part of the cycle.

There is a whole group of Bach's cantatas which do not belong to any particular cycle. These are the occasional cantatas composed for events that were not linked to the church calendar, events such as weddings, funerals, the installation of a new Council, or

1. Die St. Thomas Kirche, 2. Die Thomas Schule
3. Der Steinerne Waſſer=Kaſten.

91. Leipzig – yard of St Thomas's Church, before it was extended in 1731/32.

the dedication of a new organ. They do not differ in any special way from those written for the regular Sunday worship. Suitably for their intended function, some of them are markedly stately in character, particularly those written for the Council, for here Bach was concerned with expressing the burghers' sense of pride and self-confidence. He does this by means of more brilliant scoring, using, with the string orchestra, flutes, oboes, trumpets, and timpani. There are eleven cantatas of this kind extant, among them *Preise, Jerusalem, den Herrn* (BWV 119), written in 1723. The unknown poet draws an unmistakable parallel between Jerusalem, the symbolic seat of Christianity, and Leipzig, a town constantly admired for its natural beauty of setting amidst green meadows and woods of lime trees.

These cantatas, in whose rich variety of poetic subjects is enshrined the essence of the Christian ethic and of man's response to it, together form an artistic whole of such power and beauty that it defies comparison with any other artistic endeavour of its time. To immerse oneself in the world of these cantatas is to open the way to an historical reality which is familiar and even close to us — a reality which makes the music of Bach a part of our own life.

This is no less true for the secular cantatas, of which Bach wrote more than forty over the years. Of these, some were written for the university, the Thomasschule, or private family occasions, others for the Collegium Musicum concerts; there are also several "homage" cantatas and some that were written on commission from the court or individual members of the nobility. For many decades these secular cantatas have been overshadowed by those written for the church. In comparison with the high seriousness of the latter, their concerns seemed too trivial. The homage cantatas, especially, have been scorned for their triviality. However, the resurgence of interest in Bach's works in general has meant that more attention has been paid to these works too. And indeed, they must be considered as the equals of their sacred counterparts in the quality of their music, taking into account their very different function. In fact, the secular cantatas are greatly varied in their subject matter, and musically they contain everything that is to be found in the church cantatas apart from chorales and the type of movement based upon the chorale. A comparison of the cantatas shows that Bach made no fundamental distinction between the sacred and the secular cantata, and this point will be discussed again later.

Bach often described his secular cantatas as "dramma per musica", thereby emphasizing their similarities with opera. In matters of scoring, his cantatas certainly did not need to fear comparison with that most opulent of forms, for the forces were nearly always lavish: soloists, chorus, strings, wind, and continuo. The cantata, too, whether its role was ceremonial, congratulatory, didactic, or entertaining, was also designed to present its message in a dramatic fashion. Remarkably, the texts of the homage and congratulatory cantatas contain a message clearly based upon the bourgeois ethic of the

ARIA.

Froher Tag, verlangte Stunden,
Nun hat unfre Luft gefunden,
Was fie feft und ruhig macht.
Hier fteht unfer Schul-Gebäude,
Hier erblicket Aug und Freude
Kunft und Ordnung Zier und Pracht.

Da Capo.

Wir ftellen uns jetzt vor,
Was unfer Mufen-Chor
Vor dem vor einen Aufenthalt gehabt.
Zwar war es wohl zufrieden,
Ihm war ein Haus befchieden,

92 & 93. "Froher Tag, verlangte Stunden", cantata BWV appendix 18, text by Johann Heinrich Winkler – first edition, Leipzig, 1732.

early Enlightenment. The noble recipient of the homage or congratulation is invariably directed towards the path of justice, wisdom, or some other virtue. For example, a recitative in the birthday cantata for Prince Friedrich of Saxony, *Lasst uns sorgen, lasst uns wachen* (BWV 213) has Hercules (alias Prince Friedrich) enquiring: "Where is the right-eous path by which the innate love of virtue, glory, fame and grandeur may reach its goal? Reason, understanding and illumination require that these should all be sought. . . ." The requirements of the "dramma per musica" as specified by Bach are also fulfilled in *Der Streit zwischen Phoebus und Pan* (BWV 201). Written to a text by Picander, probably in September 1729, it was performed with the Collegium Musicum in Leipzig on Michael-mas Day at the beginning of October. A bright and entertaining work, it has a serious background. The mythological singing contest between Phoebus and Pan is a metaphor through which Bach airs his views about a fundamental problem of contemporary German music that had involved him in critical polemics over the years. It concerned the curtailment of embellishments in favour of simple melody, and while others produced learned dissertations about ornamentation Bach argued his case by composition. The two characters represent the two sides of the argument:

94. "*Schweigt stille, plaudert nicht*", *Coffee Cantata*, BWV 211 – *first page of the autograph.*

Phoebus' victory solves the conflict by demonstrating, on Bach's behalf, the right to artistic freedom. The matter was, however, rather more complicated than that. The musical characterization of Pan is not a fair reflection of the tendencies of the younger composers towards a new simplicity and naturalness, and these tendencies were to have far-reaching consequences which only became fully evident somewhat later.

Another group of secular cantatas Bach called, simply, "cantatas". These correspond more closely with the Italian chamber cantata and employ relatively small forces with no chorus. Their subjects are lyrical, contemplative, moralizing, or light-hearted. The wedding cantatas *Weichet nur, betrübte Schatten* (BWV 202) and *O holder Tag* (BWV 210) fall into this group, as does the *Coffee Cantata* (BWV 203) which is essentially an amusing chamber opera in one act. This combination of light-hearted satire and scene-painting is also to be found in the *Peasant Cantata* (BWV 212), which was written in homage to the man who had commissioned it, the chamberlain Carl Heinrich von Dieskau. The sub-title "Cantata Burlesque" draws attention to the comic aspects of the work, farmers portrayed in their own language and musical idiom, their frankness, simplicity, and cunning:

Bach's secular cantatas are a part of his vocal work which cannot be discounted. In their sureness of touch, in their relevance to life, and in their variety of form they are in no way inferior to other kinds of works. By and large their composition was not a part of Bach's official duties, but arose out of personal request or from the composer's own ideas and inventions. This is particularly true of the cantatas that were written in Leipzig. That Bach himself made no fundamental distinction between the secular and the sacred cantatas is shown by the many instances in which he turned secular cantatas into sacred works by using a different text. This procedure is called a contrafaction; it had been widespread at the time of the Reformation when the repertoire of the Protestant services had been considerably enlarged from secular sources. By no means peculiar to Bach, it is a feature of his music that remained constant throughout his life. Nor did Bach limit his use of contrafaction and parody to transforming secular works into sacred: he also practised parody within both genres by transforming instrumental music into vocal and vice versa. Some of the music was transferred note by note, but transposition, re-scoring, melodic, harmonic and thematic changes are not uncommon. The extent of Bach's reuse of material has become evident by extensive research, summarized in an interesting encyclopedic study by Norman Carroll entitled *Bach the Borrower* (1967). The parodying of vocal music sheds a particularly interesting light on the relationship between words and music. The idea that music should grow out of the words would appear to be completely at variance with the whole concept of vocal parody. In fact, the relationship between words and music is not necessarily so direct, for, as Bach showed, different words can indeed be set to the same melody without violence being done to either. This can be shown by two examples. The first is Pan's aria from *Phoebus and Pan* "Zum Tanze, zum Sprunge" which returns in the *Peasant Cantata* of 1742:

When it returns in the *Peasant Cantata* it has the same instrumentation and only a few minor note changes:

In the middle section of the aria the differences are more conspicuous, although there is still no real departure from the original:

The parody here is from one secular cantata to another. Six movements from the cantata *Lasst uns sorgen, lasst uns wachen* (BWV 213) and four from the cantata *Tönet ihr Pauken!* (BWV 214) reoccur in the Christmas Oratorio (BWV 248). The final chorus of BWV 214,

95. *Kleinzschocher near Leipzig – estate of the chamberlain, Carl Heinrich von Dieskau, where the Peasants' Cantata, BWV 212, was first performed on 30.8.1742.*

is parodied in the opening chorus of the third cantata of BWV 24:

In this instance a secular cantata has been transformed, by parody, into one for the church.

Even this necessarily brief survey of the cantatas of Bach gives some idea of the incredible breadth of Bach's creativity in this field. In no other genre did he write so many works in such a variety of forms. Unfortunately the number of works is in inverse proportion to the frequency of their performance. No other genre embraces the fundamental features of Bach's thought as comprehensively and as intricately as the cantata.

96. *"Zerreisset, zersprenget, zertrümmert die Gruft", cantata BWV 205 – first page of the autograph score.*

97. Leipzig – St Nicholas' Church, interior in the classical conversion of 1795/96.

Oratorios, Motets and Masses

In the church music of the early eighteenth century, the oratorio had a well-established place. It had originated in Italy where it was widespread by the seventeenth century and had been adopted in Germany in the time of Heinrich Schütz as a form well suited to the presentation of important themes and a significant counterpart to opera in terms of concert and church music. In the Germany of the early 1700s one of the most frequent subjects for oratorio was the story of the Passion of Jesus Christ; in many places the annual Good Friday performance of a Passion oratorio was a highlight in the musical life of the church. In Leipzig, though the forces at his disposal were not consonant with the requirements of such a large-scale work, Bach performed three of his own settings of the Passion, based respectively on the Gospels according to St John (first performed 1724), St Matthew (1727 or 1729) and St Mark (1731). The score and parts of the last-named work are lost, but music from it was parodied in various cantatas. The two surviving works stand together at the very pinnacle of the art of the German oratorio. Their musical character can be seen as a monumental elevation of the cantata, for much of their music corresponds to elements that are also found in the smaller form, yet the comparison must not be taken too far, for the subject of the Passion oratorio is of an internal and external magnitude far beyond the scope of the cantata, and this very magnitude dictates its own artistic dimensions when set to music.

Musically, the *St John Passion* (BWV 245) follows earlier German models. The parts of the text which are not taken from the Bible are clearly influenced by the Passion poem written by the Hamburg poet Berthold Heinrich Brockes which was widely known from 1712 onwards, but the actual authorship of the text is unknown; Bach edited it from various sources. The evolution of the work is particularly difficult to follow as Bach made so many changes.[10] There are two versions of the *St John Passion*, one of which was first performed in the Nikolaikirche in 1724 and the other a year later in the Thomaskirche. Bach himself, however, later returned to the 1724 version, and this is the one which is nearly always performed today.

The story of the Passion is presented in a strikingly concentrated way. Not least among Bach's concerns was that of strengthening the dramatic emphases through his music, leading to a redoubled intensification of the reality of the suffering upon the Cross, its climactic point. In 1902, Albert Schweitzer pointed out in his introduction to the *St John Passion* that Bach had made his music a counterpoint to the action, especially in the passages where the most tragic events are associated with triumphant music: "His *St John Passion* is the work of a poetic thinker expressing himself through the language of music."

The *St Matthew Passion* (BWV 244) is completely different. The text, based upon the

98. *St John Passion, BWV 245, first page of the autograph score.*

Gospel, is by Picander and was written between 1727 and 1729. Some sections of the music may be parodies of older works. So far it has been impossible to date the composition exactly and there is even uncertainty as to whether the first performance took place in 1727 or, as was formerly believed, in 1729. If any one work could be cited as the most all-embracing reflection of Bach's art, of his expressive faculty and of his ability to endow a musical structure with profound meaning, that work would be the *St Matthew Passion*. It both summarizes the development of the oratorio up to this point and lifts it to an altogether higher level; it is one of the greatest of all artistic achievements.

The theme, as in all great sacred works, can be seen as a social and human metaphor: in the sufferings of Christ are comprehended the sufferings of all mankind, and every individual can find here some reflection of private grief and its conquest, albeit raised to a sublime level. The Passion music is divided into two parts. The story begins in Part One with the Last Supper, continues with the scene on the Mount of Olives and Judas' betrayal, and ends with the arrest of Jesus. Part Two describes the examination, the sentencing to death by Pontius Pilate, the Crucifixion and the Entombment.

The textual framework is taken from St Matthew's Gospel, both for the narration and for the words of Jesus, but Picander added new texts to elaborate upon the events and provide greater depth through contemplative passages. Each addition increases the sense of personal involvement, and provides opportunities for the further enrichment of the musical setting. The numerous chorales, which act as a kind of commentary, provide pauses for reflection, for edification. The chorale melodies, which were already known to the public as congregational hymns, also provided a point of musical reference.

The recitatives in the *St Matthew Passion* have long been considered the culmination of Bach's art of musical declamation. He uses both *secco* recitative, accompanied only by the continuo, and *recitativo accompagnato*, with an orchestral accompaniment. The latter sometimes develops into arioso. The Evangelist's recitatives are all of the *secco* kind:

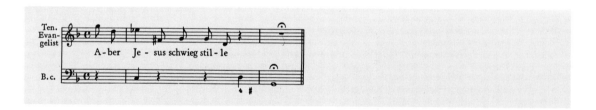

The emotional content of the words and the imagery they contain consistently determine the shape taken by the recitative. The uproar in nature with which the injustice of the Crucifixion is symbolized, becomes a dramatic, agitated recitative:

The words of Jesus are invariably in recitative and set off by a string accompaniment:

The recitatives that precede arias are often raised to the level of accompanied arioso by the vividness of the text:

As in the cantatas, Bach uses unusual combinations of forms in order to make a situation clear and in order to bring the greatest possible expressivity to bear upon it. For example, he combines recitative and chorale in alternation in No. 19 ("O Schmerz, hier zittert das gequälte Herz" for tenor solo and "Was ist die Ursach aller solcher Plagen?" for chorus), and a recitative followed by a dramatic choral outburst in No. 36 (Recit: "Und der Hohepriester antwortete", Chorus: "Er ist des Todes schuldig" . . . "Da speieten sie aus"). The arias, in their richness of emotional expression, often intensified by the use of an obbligato instrument, and their formal structure, carry their message straight to the heart. In No. 27a, a duet of lamentation for soprano and alto ("So ist mein Jesum nun gefangen"), the yearning cantilena is interrupted by surprising choral interjections, and at the end of the duet the double chorus makes very dramatic use of an *attacca* entry with "Sind Blitze, sind Donner in Wolken verschwunden". Thus does the composer build up the great, complex structures of interconnected, dramatic scenes that make of the *St Matthew Passion* a work that went far beyond anything of which the Passion oratorio, prior to 1720, had been capable.

An even greater strength was conferred on this unconventional setting of the Passion by Bach's use of two choirs and two orchestras. The very first chorus, "Kommt, ihr Töchter, helft mir klagen", with which the work opens, is a monumental chorale prelude that expands into a dimension of incomparable splendour. The entry of the unison soprano *cantus firmus* even creates the effect of a third choir. Probably at Bach's request, Picander added some lines of text so that a dialogue could be set up between the two choirs; the *cantus firmus* links them and confers an internal unity. As the story unfolds, it is punctuated twelve times by chorales, set in four parts and with *colla parte* instruments. These represent the twelve stations of the Cross. Never again was the story of the Passion

100 & 101.
Christmas Oratorio,
BWV 248 – first
edition of the text
(author unknown),
1734.

ORATORIUM,
Welches
Die heilige Weyhnacht
über
In beyden
Haupt-Kirchen
zu Leipzig
musiciret wurde.

ANNO 1734.

Am 1sten Heil. Weyhnacht-
Feyertage,
Frühe zu St. Nicolai und Nachmit-
tage zu St. Thomæ.

Tutti.

Jauchzet! frohlocket! auf! preiset
die Tage,
Rühmet, was heute der Höchste ge-
than,
Lasset das Zagen, verbannet die Klage,
Stimmet voll Jauchzen und Frö-
lichkeit an:
Dienet dem Höchsten mit herrlichen
Chören
Laßt uns den Nahmen des Höchsten
verehren.

Da Capo.

A 2   Evan-

set with such power and concentration.

Apart from the Passions, Bach wrote several other oratorios to celebrate different festivals of the church: the *Christmas Oratorio* (BWV 248), the *Easter Oratorio* (BWV 249), and the *Ascension Oratorio* (BWV 11). Of these, the last two are of less importance than the first. The Easter Oratorio *Kommt, eilet und laufet* contains no part for the Evangelist. The task of narrating the story is shared among the four solo singers. The work was fashioned into an oratorio around 1735 but had previously been an Easter cantata (*Kommt, gehet und eilet*) and even in this form had been a parody of a pastoral cantata written for the court of Weissenfels (*Entfliehet, verschwindet, entweichet, ihr Sorgen*). Picander, the author of the earliest of these texts, was probably also responsible for the text of the latest, the Easter Oratorio. The Ascension Oratorio, *Lobet Gott in seinen Reichen*, was first performed on Ascension Day 1735. The name of the poet is unknown, but it is possibly again the work of Picander. Some of the music was specially composed, some taken from at least two of Bach's previous cantatas.

Perhaps the most popular of Bach's oratorios today is the *Christmas Oratorio*. Strictly speaking, it is not an oratorio at all but a series of six cantatas based on the Christmas story and designed for the services of the first three days of Christmas, New Year's Day, the following Sunday, and Epiphany. (Bach never performed the cantatas as a single work on one day and would never have thought of doing so.) The unifying element by which the six cantatas are brought together into an oratorio-like form is supplied by the subject matter, in that they all relate to the birth of the Christ Child, and by the fact that the cantatas, although independent, fit together into an ordered whole. This is entirely consonant with our image of Bach as a composer who, time and again, not only explored a genre to its limits but redefined those limits by pushing beyond them, whether the *genre* in question was sacred or secular, vocal or instrumental. Here, in the *Christmas Oratorio*, we see Bach taking six cantatas, independent yet related in content, and reaching far beyond mere settings for services into the single entity of the oratorio. The author of the additional poetry was probably again Picander. It is very likely that Bach himself influenced the choice of the words and chorales and had a say in the manner in which they were assembled as well as in the arrangement of the additional poetry. Considered as an entity, the work richly fulfils every requirement of the oratorio of its time (around 1735). The six parts (which in the context of the oratorio can be seen as two parts each consisting of three sections, "Part One" relating to Christmas, "Part Two" to the New Year) are so structurally organized from one climax to another that there is total unity within their variety, which was entirely congruent with the demands of the contemporary oratorio.

Every section opens with a differently-worked choral movement, though Part Two is prefaced by an expressive sinfonia for the Shepherds and Angels. Each section closes with a chorale, although the third section is rounded off (after the chorale) with a reprise of the opening chorus. Every time, Bach finds a different formal solution for the final chorale: interludes with trumpets, with woodwind, with a festive orchestral ritornello, with an unadorned four-part chorus, and, finally, with the full chorus and orchestra combining in a splendid, brilliant movement with a solo trumpet. Thus does the composer avoid the danger of uniformity that was inherent in a series of six cantatas: finding different formal solutions and continually bringing in some new and contrasting element. In the vocal sections, too, the *da capo* form is constantly varied by melodic invention and enriched by dance rhythms, virtuosic treatment and ever-varying obbligati. The sequence is also varied by the use of the duet (Part III, No. 29) and the trio (Part VI, No. 51). The simple recitatives of the Evangelist have immediacy and sincerity. All the recitatives are enlivened by a variety of methods, such as the interweaving of chorale and recitative (for example in No. 7, "Er ist auf Erden kommen arm"), the introduction of dialogue (No. 13 "Und der Engel sprach zu ihnen"), or even by using all four soloists in a four-part arioso (No. 63).

In this synthesis of six cantatas Bach has put three decades of experience in cantata composition. That the *Christmas Oratorio* should have made so much use of parody is remarkable, as is the fact that a large proportion of the parodied material was predominantly of secular origin. Among the cantatas that served him so well were those that he had written for members of the family of the Elector in Dresden: *Tönet, ihr Pauken!* (BWV 214) and *Lasst uns sorgen, lasst uns wachen* (BWV 213). The introductory chorus from BWV 214 was transformed from *Tönet, ihr Pauken!* into *Jauchzet, frohlocket*, the introductory chorus to Part I of the *Christmas Oratorio*; the bass aria "Kron' und Preis gekrönter Damen" became "Grosser Herr und starker König" and the alto aria "Fromme Musen! Meine Glieder!" became the tenor aria "Frohe Hirten eilt, ach eilt". Like countless other examples of parody, these make us aware that it would be a mistake to consider the relationship between words and music in the Baroque era immutable; parody was widely practised. In putting one melody with different texts of very different import, the major consideration was that of the suitability of the verse form. The number of syllables and the structure of the stanza had to be compatible. Given this condition, the words of a parody cantata can have a totally different significance from those of the original but the music can remain unaltered or only very slightly changed. Thus, the F major duet for Hercules and Virtue (alto and tenor) in BWV 213 has the following text: "I am yours and you are mine!/I kiss you, and you kiss me!" which reappears in the *Christmas Oratorio* as a duet for soprano and bass, transposed into A major and accompanied by oboes d'amore instead of violas, as: Lord, thy pity and thy mercy/ shall console us, set us free".

In contrast to many works by Bach, the *Christmas Oratorio* does not seem to have fallen into complete neglect after the composer's death. In 1764 the parts were offered to Breitkopf, the Leipzig music publishers, and it seems that isolated performances were given here and there. (C. P. E. Bach directed a performance of this work in 1778, calling it "Music for Easter", presumably with some changes. But it is only within the last few decades that the *Christmas Oratorio* has established its position in the concert repertoire, largely owing to the efforts of Karl Straube and Günther Ramin, two Thomascantors.

Yet even Albert Schweitzer, in his *J. S. Bach*, in 1907, was recommending "considerable cutting", and for decades there was a quite one-sided preference for the first three cantatas that is only gradually being rectified by complete performances of all six whether performed in a single concert or spread out over two. The same is true both for the *St Matthew Passion* and the *Mass in B minor*, of which uncut performances are now becoming more and more a matter of course.

In the magnitude of their theme and the complexity of their treatment, the Passions and the *Christmas Oratorio* occupy the dominant place in Bach's sacred music. They went beyond the limits which had been heretofore established for Protestant liturgical music and were, at the same time, testaments to a wholly unshaken faith. The entire history of Protestant sacred music contains nothing which can claim superiority over the oratorios of Bach. Birth and suffering: these were the themes, in short, to which Bach, by his music, gave a human face. Within the oratorios Bach combines the traditions of Lutheran church music (especially the central one of the chorale) with an advanced approach: old-style polyphony is permeated by cantilena and expressive writing, by which the form is renewed and carried beyond the narrow definition of church music.

Every performance of a Passion was an important event in the life of the church and called for maximum exertion. It could cause friction, too, especially when Bach found his plans frustrated by his superiors. On one occasion, when the Leipzig town council banned the performance of a Passion (in 1739), he remarked with bitter indifference that he would get nothing out of it and that it would be "only a burden".

Every musical *genre* has its own individual history. Even given the close interdependence of words and music imposed by the liturgical function of church music, the forms employed were not impervious to change. The motet is a case in point. Since the sixteenth century, the motet had played an important, even dominating, role in the vocal music of the German Protestant church. In the seventeenth century, the polyphonic character of the motet acquired a wholly new range of expression by adopting, from

102. B minor Mass, BWV 232 – opening of the Kyrie, soprano 1, autograph.

Der Marckt in Leipzig

monody, the prominent treble line with basso continuo accompaniment, and, from the early concerto, the principle of contrast, of dialogue. However, this development was eventually to prove fatal to the motet, for it was the immediate cause of the rise of the sacred concerto and the cantata, which caused a gradual decline in the art of motet writing in Germany. When Bach started his work in Leipzig, motets had been a traditional part of the repertoire of the choir.[11] Its Golden Age was, however, already in decline. Bach had long been familiar with the motet, which had been at the very heart of church music during his childhood and early adulthood. Several motets are to be found in the "Alt-Bachische Archiv", a collection of works by members of the Bach family which was initiated by Johann Ambrosius Bach and continued by Johann Sebastian, his son. When Bach was in Leipzig, motets were usually required for services for the dead. We now know that all Bach's motets were, with one exception, composed before the early 1730s. Those for double choir are: *Singt dem Herrn ein neues Lied* (BWV 225), *Der Geist hilft unser Schwachheit auf* (BWV 226), *Fürchte dich nicht* (BWV 228) and *Komm, Jesu komm!* (BWV 229). Those for a single choir, with from three to five parts are: *Jesu, meine Freude* (BWV 227), *Lobet den Herrn, alle Heiden* (BWV 230) and *O Jesu Christ, mein's Lebens Licht* (BWV 231).

It was believed for a long time that the motets were intended to be performed unaccompanied, but this theory is now in doubt. There is an extant autograph of *Der Geist hilft unser Schwachheit auf* with parts for four stringed instruments (first chorus), two oboes, *taille* and bassoon (second chorus) and continuo of organ and bass viol. This suggests that the instruments doubled the vocal parts, supporting the singers which, given the technical difficulty of the music, was of considerable help. *A cappella* singing in the late Baroque was rare and the singers were not used to it. Bach himself added a basso continuo to Palestrina's Missa brevis. Since motets were normally performed at a memorial service which was held before the actual day of burial, they would have to be written and rehearsed in a comparatively short time, and there was therefore good reason for using the instruments. But the only church in Leipzig that permitted the use of instruments at times of mourning and for funeral services was the Paulinerkirche. Hence the continuing debate over the use of instruments in motets, and hence the theory that they may have been used on other occasions apart from the services for the dead.

Compared with Bach's prolific output in other vocal genres, the number of motets (seven) is small; nevertheless, their quality confers upon them a position of quite exceptional importance, and they represent the highest peak of the form's post-Renaissance

103. Leipzig – the celebration of Friedrich August II's accession, the market place, 21.4.1733.

141

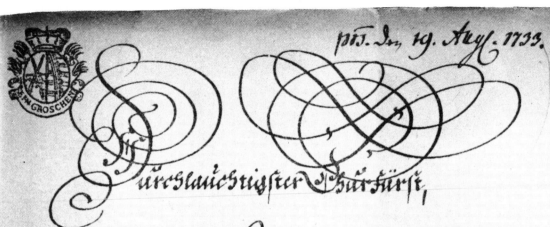

Durchlauchtigster Churfürst,

Gnädigster Herr,

Ew. Königl. Hoheit überreiche in tiefster Devotion gegenwärtige geringe Arbeit von derjenigen Wissenschaft, welche ich in der Musique erlanget, mit gantz unterthänigster Bitte, Sie wollen dieselbe nicht nach der schlechten Composition, sondern nach Dero Welt berühmten Clemenz mit gnädigsten Augen ansehen, und mich dabey in Dero mächtigste Protection zu nehmen geruhen. Ich habe einige Jahre und bis daher bey denen beyden Haupt-Kirchen in Leipzig das Directorium in der Music gehabt, dabey aber ein und andere Bekränkung unverschuldeter dinge, iezuweilen auch Verminderung derer mit dieser Function verknüpften Accidentien empfinden müssen, welches aber gäntz

development. Nearly all of them, naturally, make use of the chorale, either by the employment of a single chorale verse, as in *Der Geist hilft unser Schwachheit auf* or by the use of a series of verses which provide the music and the significance of the whole, as in *Jesu, meine Freude*. In only one case, that of *Lobet den Herrn, alle Heiden*, is a short Psalm substituted for the chorale.

The connection between words and music had always been especially close in the motet, where opportunities for expressive interpretation were frequent and gave the composer ample opportunity to display his skill in declamatory and rhetorical writing. In this respect, as well as in the combination of elaborate linear polyphony with homophonic writing, Bach's motets demonstrate abundantly the expressive and virtuosic possibilities inherent in the form. It is no coincidence that they make outstanding demands on the vocal and expressive capabilities of a choir.

Since the Lutheran Reformation, the use of German as the language of the church had superseded Latin, which gradually fell into disuse. The sung liturgy, accordingly, was more and more frequently performed in German so that the common people could understand the meaning of the words. However, many Latin texts had achieved an important status in evangelical Protestantism, and in the Leipzig of Bach's time parts of the services were still, on occasion, performed in Latin including sections of the Mass on certain festivals and the Magnificat. Bach often used other composers' Lutheran Masses for performance, but he also contributed four of them (BWV 233–236); however, these were all *contrafacta* made from earlier cantatas. All these works were overshadowed by the *Mass in B minor* (BWV 232).[12] This was destined to be the last major choral work that Bach completed, but was also a summation of his experience in the field of vocal composition. It is worth pausing for a moment to describe the evolution of this great work and to give some account of its artistic splendour.

We have already mentioned that in 1733, Bach petitioned the new Elector of Saxony for a court title. He accompanied his request with manuscript parts of a Missa brevis in B minor. It is possible that the two movements of this Missa brevis had been performed during the service of ascension of Friedrich August II in Leipzig. In his accompanying letter Bach wrote:

> To Your Royal Highness I offer in profound devotion this slight work, a result of that knowledge and skill that I have acquired in music. . . . For some years, and up to this present moment, I have held the Directorium of music in both the principal churches of Leipzig, but, although innocent, have had to suffer many an injury of one sort or another including a decrease in those fees which should accrue to me in this office; but all these injuries could be quite discounted if Your Royal Highness were to favour me with a title in your Court Capelle and to issue the appropriate decree; . . . and I offer my most grateful service to show obedience at all times, upon Your Royal Highness's most gracious desire, in the composition of music both for the church and the orchestra . . .

Having been known to the court at Dresden for years, Bach had every reason to suppose that his hopes stood a good chance of fulfilment; but he had to wait until the end of November 1736 before receiving the news that the Elector had decided to honour him only with the title of Court Composer. In the meantime the bitter dispute over the prefects had worsened his relations with the Leipzig Town Council and the Thomasschule. It was not until nearly fifteen years later (*c.* 1747–48) that Bach added the rest of the Mass to the Kyrie and Gloria.

In its complete form the *Mass in B minor* is not suitable for liturgical use in either Catholic or Protestant church, and it is unlikely that Bach himself ever heard it in full. We do not know whether it was his intention, in 1733, to extend the Kyrie and Gloria

104. Letter written by J. S. Bach on 27.7.1733 to Friedrich August II, to accompany the vocal parts of the Mass – first page of the autograph.

into a "Missa tota"; it seems more probable that he only took this decision after 1740, the epoch when he was particularly involved with collecting and completing works. He also saw himself at this time as the guardian of the great traditions of the past surrounded by the "modern" composers of the fast-growing new style no longer devoted to polyphony. The creation of a large work that would serve as an example and a model would have seemed a natural thing to do. It is a synthesis of the powerful musical suggestion of the Latin text and Bach's own lifelong experience of expressing intense subjective emotions, and while not one movement denies the tradition to which it belongs, it reaches beyond the confine of that tradition and certainly beyond the normal bounds of the Liturgy in terms of technical demands, scoring, and length. It is unlikely, however, that this aspect had any determining influence upon Bach: his intention was patently to realize a work of all-embracing dimensions that sprang directly from his own creative urge. This is confirmed by the character of Bach's works in the last decade of his life and above all by his tendency to plan his output over a period of time.

The Mass consists of the usual five parts of the Ordinary: Kyrie, Gloria, Credo, Sanctus, Agnus Dei. Each of these five parts is rich and complex in structure and contains various sections which, in their style and their instrumentation, reveal a dramatic form which has been thought through to the last detail. Nevertheless, the architecture of the huge work has recently been questioned, for it is very difficult to arrive at a convincing analysis since the *B minor Mass* is a cantata Mass, i.e. it is made up of a string of cantatas like the Christmas Oratorio. Moreover, as we have already noted, with a few exceptions they are parodies of earlier cantatas. Bach was able to give full rein to his predilection for splendid sonorities and choral grandeur in such movements as the opening Kyrie, for these were characteristic features of Catholic church music of the Baroque era:

Expressive cantabile, long a characteristic of Bach's cantatas and oratorios, is prevalent in the solo vocal numbers and solo ensembles in which obbligato instruments such as the violin, flute, oboe d'amore and corno da caccia partner the human voice. Vocal and instrumental sections are thematically linked:

In this aria the role of the violin is decidedly virtuosic: by soaring up to e‴, the very top of its range at the time (*c.* 1740), its song of praise becomes not only figurative but a veritable emulation of the song of the angels in heaven. The movements in which Bach uses orchestra and chorus in a joyful and exultant confession of faith are of a thrilling musical power. An example of this is the "Et resurrexit" (He is risen), a movement which originated in a birthday cantata for August II. The concertante style is reminiscent of the kind of opening chorus he used so often for cantatas.

This type of joyful *éclat* is counterbalanced by the grieving sublimity of the Crucifixus. Here the forces are much reduced. Descending chromatic motifs

are linked to calls of lamentation:

Characteristically, there is nothing maudlin about this mourning. It is controlled, almost objective, and raised above a mere personal level. The fact remains, though, that this quality was present in the cantata from which the Crucifixus was taken.

The structure of the Mass is tightened by the use of large-scale formal devices, as, for instance, the symmetrical form of the Credo, in which the Crucifixus acts as the pivotal point towards which and away from which the rest of the movement radiates.

The music of the Gratias in Part II (Gloria) returns in the final section of the last part, the Dona nobis pacem. In Bach's work nothing is done without a good reason. Here, the music of thanksgiving returns as a prayer for peace, illustrating the association of prayer and fulfilment. This is a highly concentrated movement, in which every note has its predetermined, logical place and nothing is extraneous, nothing extravagant:

105. Dresden, etching by Alexander Thiele, 1726

A movement such as this should not be seen solely as an expression of religious faith, but as a testimony to Bach's thought as a whole. The end of the work, a section full of optimism, is an image of Bach's conception not only of God but of the world as well. Life and faith are seen as a whole, belief becomes the mainspring of action, and music enshrines man's capacity for both in an aura of grandeur and beauty.

106. Violin by Christian Hoffmann, Leipzig 1729. Flute. by Johann Heinrich Eichentopf, Leipzig, c.1730.

Chamber Music and the Art of Fugue

Instrumental chamber music was widely practised in early eighteenth-century Germany as a social form of music-making in the home. The sonata for various string and wind instruments with continuo accompaniment prevailed. Sonatas or suites for a single unaccompanied instrument were more rare, but the trio sonata for two solo instruments and continuo had had a wide currency since the late seventeenth century.

As far as can be ascertained today, most of Bach's chamber music was written during the Cöthen period. Reliable documentary evidence relating to his work in Weimar is not available. Two groups of chamber works are outstanding as models of their genres: the sonatas for a solo instrument (violin, flute, viola da gamba) with keyboard accompaniment, and the works for unaccompanied solo instruments (sonatas and partitas for violin, suites for cello).

Chamber music appeals first and foremost to the connoisseur and active amateur musician, thus the composer is free to set himself specific targets without having to consider the taste of the general public. Two types of sonata with several movements were well-established in the early eighteenth century: the chamber sonata (*sonata da camera*), which had developed from the suite and had three movements (fast–slow–fast) and the church sonata (*sonata da chiesa*) which was sometimes played during the service and had four movements (slow–fast–slow–fast). Both originated in Italy and had been brought to Germany in the mid-seventeenth century.

For chamber music with keyboard Bach favoured the four-movement form and even extended it on two occasions. But in only six of his sonatas did he use the keyboard instrument as a continuo: in the sonatas for violin in G major and E minor (BWV 1021 and 1023), the three sonatas for flute (BWV 1033–1035) and the sonatas for two flutes (BWV 1039). Here Bach employs the old monodic style of putting all the melodic emphasis on to the violin or flute and consigning the keyboard to an accompanying role:

Remembering the pioneering work that Bach did in freeing the keyboard from its role as a mere continuo instrument and elevating it to the rank of a solo instrument, it is not surprising that this attitude is also reflected in his chamber works. In the majority of them the keyboard is a full partner of the melody instrument and has its share of thematic material and technical difficulty. The texture of the sonatas is an interweaving of three strands, the line of the melody instrument and the two obbligato keyboard lines. This was an innovation that led specifically to the development of chamber music with an independent keyboard part. Nevertheless, upon close examination we see that these are still really trio sonatas, the right hand part of the harpsichord being the second voice of the trio sonata.

Works of this type include the six sonatas for violin (BWV 1014–1019), the three sonatas for viola da gamba (BWV 1027–1029) and the three sonatas for flute (BWV 1030–1032).

107. Sonata in B minor for flute and obbligato harpsichord – opening of the Largo, autograph.

The collection of six works for, respectively, unaccompanied violin and unaccompanied cello date from around 1720. There are three sonatas and three partitas for solo violin (BWV 1001–1006) and six suites for solo cello (BWV 1007–1012). All twelve works hold a very special position of pre-eminence in the literature of works for solo string instruments. In composing these works Bach was continuing a German tradition. Some of his predecessors in the genre were known to Bach personally, such as Paul von Westhoff in Weimar and Johann Georg Pisendel in Dresden. The three solo sonatas are again in four movements. The slow opening movements have certain features of the fantasia and elements of improvisation as is shown in the rich ornamentation that Bach wrote out with great precision:

In all three sonatas the second movement is a fugue. In BWV 1003 and 1005 the fugues are of much greater length than one would expect in a work of this kind, being of 289 and 354 bars respectively. In the first sonata, in G minor (BWV 1001), the third movement is a *siciliano*, a dance form more usually found in the suite. The final movements, respectively presto, allegro and allegro arioso, are emphatically brilliant and virtuosic.

In the three partitas the highly stylized, dance-like elements of the suite predominate. The basic model of the suite is realized and developed differently in each of the three works:

I Allemande — *Double* — Courante — *Double* — Sarabande — *Double* — Bourrée — *Double*.
II Allemande — Courante — Sarabande — Gigue — Ciacona.
III Prelude — Loure — Gavotte en rondeau — Menuett I — Menuett II — Bourrée — Gigue.

The third partita is the only one to be introduced by a prelude, a movement not normally found in the suite. All six works, the three sonatas and the three partitas, explore the potentialities of their forms, combining traditional elements with an unmistakable individuality. These works demonstrate in an entirely exemplary way Bach's ability to solve the problem of polyphonic writing for a single melody instrument, an ability which undoubtedly owes much to his own skill as a violinist. They all make extremely heavy technical demands on the player and display an almost limitless imagination in spite of the restrictions of the genre. They contain genuine harmonic writing in the chords:

and even genuine polyphonic part-writing:

and there are passages in which Bach deploys the single line in such a way as to create the illusion of two-part writing:

By techniques such as these, and many others besides, Bach creates a harmonic texture from which he draws the strongly differentiated effects of the pieces. The ciacona (chaconne) in BWV 1004 is one of the finest variation works that he ever wrote. Like the Organ Passacaglia in C minor (BWV 582) and the *Goldberg Variations* (BWV 988) it reveals his inexhaustible capacity for transforming musical ideas.

Each of the six suites for solo cello begins with a prelude. The other movements are all dance forms and follow the basic pattern of Allemande — Courante — Sarabande — Gigue, into which Bach inserts Menuetts I and II, Bourrées I and II or Gavottes I and II before the final movement.

The works for unaccompanied solo strings have always been regarded as especially searching tests of performing skill and are referred to as such by Forkel in his Bach biography. However, the virtuosic technical aspects, essential as they may be to these remarkable works, are of much less significance than their sheer artistic value, and it is no coincidence that these pieces, which form a veritable encyclopedia of solo string playing,

108. Silbermann fortepiano – played by Bach on his visit to Potsdam, 7.5.1747.

should have retained their special status in the literature for these instruments.

When in mid-May 1747, Bach returned from his visit to the Prussian court, he completed a work based on the "royal theme" that had been given him by Frederick the Great. This project, which became the "Humble offering of thanks to His Majesty King Frederick II" — in other words the *Musical Offering* — became extremely ambitious, and was eventually presented to the king in July of the same year with the following letter of dedication:

> Most gracious King,
> With all due humility I dedicate to Your Royal Majesty this Musical Offering, of which the noblest part is the work of your own august hand. I still remember with reverential pleasure the very special royal grace with which, on the occasion of my visit to Potsdam some time ago, Your Royal Majesty in person played for me a theme for a fugue upon the clavier and charged me most graciously to carry it out in Your Own august Presence. To obey Your Majesty's command was my humble duty. I very soon perceived, however, that because of the lack of necessary preparation, the execution was not doing justice to the excellence of the theme. I resolved, therefore, and promptly pledged myself to work out this right Royal Theme fully and thereafter to make it known to the world. This project has now been fulfilled to the best of my abilities, with no other end in view than the irreproachable intention of glorifying, even if only in small measure, the fame of a Monarch whose greatness and power, as in all the arts and sciences of war and peace, so especially in music, has won the admiration and respect of all men. I make so bold as to add this most humble prayer: That Your Majesty may graciously deign to accept this slight work, and continue to grant Your Majesty's most august Royal grace to
>   Your Majesty's
>   most humble and dutiful servant,
>   the Author.

The edition was published complete in 1747 and put on sale at Michaelmas.[13] An announcement in a Leipzig newspaper of 30 September gives the following information about the contents of the work: "This elaborate study consists of 1) two fugues, one with three, the other with six obbligato parts; 2) a sonata for flute, violin and continuo; 3) various canons including a canonic fugue." The compilation is most unusual in the disparity of its parts, but they are all linked by their dependence upon the royal theme.

This reveals the specific purpose of the work. As was the case in other works or collections of works, Bach's original aim, in this instance that of writing a "fugue", seems to have changed. He apparently decided that he wished to demonstrate comprehensively his ability and skill, and did so by elaborating upon the King's theme in a variety of ways. Beside the keyboard fugues of ricercars, in three and six parts respectively, the canon comes into its own in nine different versions. Given their imitative character, both fugue (ricercar) and canon are ideally suited to explore the manifold potentialities of a theme, thus demonstrating not only the composer's practical experience but also, to an equal degree, his scholarship and his imagination. This was Bach's aim.

In the *Musical Offering*, Bach took Frederick the Great's considerable musical accomplishments into account, including a trio sonata for flute, violin and continuo for the flautist-King. Its form is that of the four-movement *sonata da chiesa*. Although based on the "royal theme", it differs from the other pieces in being written in the modern style fashionable at the court, and with expressive cantabile:

Whereas Bach clearly intended that the fugues should be performed on a keyboard instrument, there are two places in the canons where there are indications for the addition of flute and violin. This is the same scoring as for the trio sonata. In the case of canons it had been quite usual for the composer not to indicate specifically the entries of separate instruments, and this put the onus of scholarship on to the musicians themselves. Bach emphasizes the scholarly aspect by using Latin for the titles of the canons and for the little poetic maxims that he adds to the score, such as: "Notulis crescendibus cresceat Fortuna Regis" ("As the music waxes, so shall the happiness of the King"). For the printed edition Bach prefaced the six ricercars and the ten *canones diversi* with an acrostic, a play on words in which, by taking the first letter of each word, the key-word may be discovered: "Regis Iussi Cantio Et Reliqua Canonica Arte Resoluta" (the movement composed at the King's command and the remainder worked out by means of the art of canon). The movement the King required is the RICERCAR — the fugue.

There is nothing to suggest that Bach intended his *Musical Offering* to be performed as a cycle. As far as the canons are concerned, practical considerations of performance are hardly in evidence: they may be seen first and foremost as models of polyphonic scholarship. One's attention is constantly directed towards the fundamental aim of the work, which was to establish on the written page the working-out of a theme that had been originally improvised, making multiple use of the scholarly imitative forms of ricercar and canon as well as including a trio sonata in which the flute part was cleverly devised for the King and whose expressivity provides proof of Bach's equal mastery of traditional and contemporary styles. The total concept reflects Bach's predilection for comprehensiveness in his works which is also evident in many other compositions and collections of works.

A further example of this predilection is to be found in his last, uncompleted work, *The Art of Fugue* (BWV 1080). Although this is not a chamber work, it is included here for reasons which will become clear later. In no other genre did Bach prove his authority more impressively or demonstrate his dialectical relationship with tradition more successfully than in the fugue. For him the fugue was not only a genre in the sense of a type of form, but was also an intellectual principle of composition to be used as a formal device in many different genres — masses, motets, oratorios, cantatas, chorale settings, concertos, sonatas, suites, etc. The fugue was also the embodiment of musical scholarship, of master-craftsmanship. As Scheibe's criticism of Bach showed, to the younger generation around 1730 it represented the music of yesterday, but Bach was able to find ways of introducing new elements, of conferring an individual character upon it, and, by loosening its historical frontiers, to bring it into a new perspective.

There was, then, no lack of logic in his adding to the collections he had already made — the *Clavier-Übung*, and *Well Tempered Clavier*, the Chorale settings and the *Musical Offering* — one which was, in effect, a summation of his life's work bequeathed to his contemporaries and successors. His entry into Mizler's Society in June 1747 may have further stimulated his work; it may even have been intended to be submitted to the Society as the annual contribution of a work that was required of every member.

In basing his work on a single theme, Bach's aim was to demonstrate the various forms of the fugue. He stressed the "scholarly" aspect of the work by using the old nomenclature "contrapunctus". Strikingly enough, there are four canons included in the work, and, as in the *Musical Offering*, fugues and canons are directly linked to one another. It would seem that in Bach's time, the forms in which the all-important principle of imitation was predominant were considered to be linked much more closely than they were in later years.

In Contrapunctus I the theme is presented:

It is then worked out in straightforward fugues, counter-fugues, double fugues, triple fugues, mirror fugues, four canons and an unfinished quadruple fugue. The last of these breaks off where Bach began to use a theme based on his own name (B in German musical notation corresponds to our B flat, and the German H to our B natural):

It is not known exactly when Bach began work on *The Art of Fugue*, but the most recent research by Christoph Wolff, based on an examination of the writing and the paper, dates a considerable part of it in the early 1740s. Thus work on it must have been spread over some years, and its genesis must have overlapped other works of the last decade of Bach's life. The date at which he stopped composing *The Art of Fugue* is equally uncertain. Towards the end the trouble with his eyes made him totally dependent upon amanuenses. It is therefore impossible to say whether the work would have ended with the quadruple fugue or whether more canons would have been included.

As was the case with the *Musical Offering*, the title *The Art of Fugue* was not used by Bach himself in his original autograph. It was appended to the work for the first time in 1751 in an advertisement for subscribers and immediately copied by Friedrich Wilhelm Marpurg when he produced the first printed edition in April/May 1752. In this edition a chorale setting ("Wenn wir in höchsten Nöten sein") was added to the unfinished quadruple fugue. Bach had dictated this to his son-in-law Altnickol on his sick-bed, but it has nothing to do with *The Art of Fugue*. A printed message to the purchasers stated that it should be considered as "compensation" for the unfinished state of the Fugue.

For many years *The Art of Fugue* was the subject of considerable speculation both on account of its incompleteness and the uncertainty about its origins. There is no longer any need for this. It is the work of a composer who periodically sought to summarize his musical experience in a continuous process of self-realization which carried him towards a greater understanding of his art. He reached the point where he no longer needed the direct stimulus of an external commission but could draw solely upon his own resources. Bach had developed the capacity to work in such a way over many years, and had shown the first overt signs of it at the time of the publication of the *Clavier-Übung*, which was by its very nature a statement of artistic emancipation. In the individuality of its form, *The Art of Fugue* was a kind of apotheosis of the fugue. It was a blend of practical experience, tradition, scholarly penetration, and a firm grasp of the very stuff of music and its contemporary potentialities. The result of such a blend was a work of truly encyclopedic proportions.

Da Vorzeiger dieses Hr. Christian Friedrich
Schemelli hiesiger Studiosus mich umb Bekandt=
schaft, Ihm wegen bezeigten fleisses in
Musicis ein attestat: zu ertheilen; Als habe
Ihme solches nicht abschlagen, sondern vielmehr
bezeigen sollen, wie er indeßzeit, so lange er
unserer Schule zu S. Thomas frequentiret
alle mögliche fleiß darinne erwiesen, daß
Ihn auch bey denen Cantoreyen als Sopranist
gantz wohl habe gebrauchen können.

Leipzig. d. 24. Febr. 1740.

Johann Sebast: Bach.
Königl: Pohl. u. ChurfL:
Sächß. HofCompositeur.

The Teacher

J ohann Sebastian Bach lived in an age that was devoting an ever-increasing amount of attention to education. The decades immediately before and and after 1700 not only saw a significant improvement in popular education, but the emergance of a desire to collate, classify and disseminate all kinds of knowledge, including all the available knowledge about music. This was all part of the early stages of the Enlightenment in Germany, principally affecting the middle classes but also promoted enthusiastically by many princes and other aristocrats. In the predominantly Catholic countries such as France, the Enlightenment was bound up with strong anti-religious and anti-clerical attitudes but the Protestant countries, where the Lutheran Reformation had already brought about significant constitutional changes, saw a development that was less antagonistic towards religion; by and large a belief in God was associated with the most positive values of the Enlightenment, its concern with knowledge, education, understanding, justice and humanity. Bach had met with attitudes of this kind since his earliest days in Thuringia; they had been prevalent in Cöthen, and accepted as a matter of course in Leipzig, one of the largest and most influential centres of urban bourgeois life and culture in central Germany.

It is most important that we should see Bach's activities as a teacher within the context of the enlightened educational climate that prevailed in Northern Germany.

As an organist, Cantor, Konzertmeister and Kapellmeister, Bach had always had teaching responsibilities in the broader sense, through his involvement with the coaching, training, and rehearsing of singers and instrumentalists. The formal teaching of large groups was another matter: the problems he encountered as a young organist with the schoolboy choristers in Arnstadt, the lengths to which he went to avoid teaching Latin at the Thomasschule, and the considerable problems of discipline that he had at this school all seem to show him up as a not very capable pedagogue. It is probable that his irascible temperament made him unsuitable for such work. On the other hand, working as a musician among musicians, his outstanding skills and experience must have given him all the necessary authority as well as the ability to inspire his singers and instrumentalists with all the self-confidence they could possibly require. If this were not the case, his decades of work as Cantor and Kapellmeister and the standards that he required of, and achieved with, his musicians, would be unimaginable.

Bach's accomplishments as a teacher are seen more clearly in two other areas of that activity: as a teacher of private pupils, and as the composer of works with a primarily didactic aim. Pupils flocked to learn from him, and between 1707 and the end of his life he personally taught no less than eighty of them. Of these, some came from Thuringian families known to the Bachs, some were recommended by other teachers and others were drawn by his mighty reputation alone. His first pupil was Johann Martin Schubert, who came to him in 1707 in Mühlhausen. Schubert was only five years younger than Bach and had been born in the village of Geraberg near Ilmenau. When the Bachs moved from Mühlhausen to Weimar Schubert moved with them and continued his studies of the organ and keyboard instruments, and on Bach's relinquishing the Weimar post his pupil succeeded him as court musician and organist. He died in April 1721, at an early age. Another of Bach's pupils in Weimar was Johann Caspar Vogler, who became organist of Stadtilm in 1715 and succeeded Schubert in Weimar in 1721, even becoming mayor there in 1735. The following is a representative selection of Bach's later pupils:

> Johann Gotthilf Ziegler (1688–1747)
> Joh. Georg Schübler (born c.1720)
> Heinrich Nicolaus Gerber (1702–1775)
> Joh. Ludwig Krebs (1713–1780)
> Georg Friedrich Einicke (1710–1770)
> Joh. Elias Bach (1705–1755)
> Joh. Friedrich Doles (1715–1797)
> Joh. Friedrich Kittel (1732–1809)
> Johann Gottfried Müthel (1728–1788)

Not least among his pupils were his own sons, and in as much as he taught them all to sing and instructed them in the general arts of making music, his whole family too should be counted. Since Bach's pupils found employment all over Germany and in other countries too, and since they continued to keep in contact with him over the years and to make copies of his works, they constitute a bridge between him and the latter half of the eighteenth century, even into the early years of the nineteenth. As a consequence of having received their musical education at his hands, they transmitted his influence, his experience and his philosophy to future generations despite the essentially different attitudes towards art and style that, as members of a younger generation, they inevitably adopted. Thus, the number and quality of Bach's pupils ensured that his work did not fall into complete oblivion. Much has been written about the comparative neglect of his works in the period immediately following his death, and it is a fact that only isolated fragments of it were known; his greatest achievements had to wait until the nineteenth century before being rediscovered.

In considering Bach as a teacher we must also take into account the substantial body of compositions that he produced with didactic aims specifically in mind. A whole series of collections of works for organ and keyboard demonstrate his aims both by their content and by the comments that he appended to them in accordance with a well-established tradition. Detailed informative titles, often linked to a dedication, clarify the intentions of the composer and demonstrate the close relationship between composer, performer, teacher and pupil. This is illustrative of the didactic turn of mind which became more and more effective as, during the course of Bach's life, the demand for knowledge, education and enlightenment became increasingly insistent.

It was in Weimar that Bach assembled the manuscripts for the *Orgelbüchlein*. His original plan was that it should contain 118 chorale preludes, one for each day of the ecclesiastical year, in their correct sequence. The title page (which gives no date of composition) informs us of the aims of the collection and also about Bach's readiness to see himself in the role of a teacher:

Little Notebook for the Organ in which the beginner on the organ is instructed in how to develop a chorale in many different ways and may at the same time acquire facility

in the use of the pedals, since in the chorales contained herein the pedal is treated as wholly obbligato. Glory to be to God on high/And may my neighbour learn thereby. . . .

Bach is here turning his attention to the beginner, an experienced composer and performer sharing his knowledge usefully with his pupils. He is concerned not merely with a certain kind of chorale prelude but with its various potentialities, and he avoids strict rules. He wants, too, to show how the chorale can be played "in many different ways". He lays great stress on the use of the pedals, yet despite the acknowledged intention to teach pedal technique, the chorales are not limited in their suitability for use in church. His method of teaching the use of the pedals was by treating them quite independently from the keyboard, "wholly obbligato", thus achieving a balance, a musical partnership between foot and hand which will result in the full use of the instrument with all its polyphonic possibilities. As was to be expected, Bach ends with an affirmation of his faith and with the hope that his work will benefit his fellow men.

For reasons that have never come to light, Bach never completed this collection. As it stands, and with later additions, it includes forty-six chorale preludes, enough for the pupil to aim at realizing the intentions of the composer.

In 1722 Bach completed *The Well Tempered Clavier* in Cöthen. Twenty-two years later a second, similar, collection followed. On the title page of 1722, which he wrote himself, Bach again presents himself as both teacher and composer:

The Well Tempered Clavier, or, Preludes and Fugues through all the tones and semitones both as regards the *tertia major* or Do-Re-Mi and the *tertia minor* or Re-Mi-Fa, for the use and profit of young people desirous of studying music, and as a pastime for those already skilled in this study, prepared and completed by Joh. Sebastian Bach. . . .

The scheme of the work had been suggested by the age-old problem of the tuning of instruments. The harmonically pure tuning that had been in use until the end of the seventeenth century led to an increasing impurity of the intervals the further one got away from the key of C major. The only really practical keys were those with a maximum of three sharps or three flats. Since the early seventeenth century various solutions had been suggested without success. Then in 1680/1 Andreas Werckmeister published his findings about the possibility of tuning instruments according to a new, "well-tempered" system that allowed previously unusable tonalities to be employed. Bach, like some others of his contemporaries, seized upon this important innovation and designed his collection of preludes and fugues so that the player could master the technical aspects of all the keys, hence "Preludes and Fugues through *all* the tones and semitones". To make the situation clear, he explains further that he intends to include both major and minor "thirds". He tells us, moreover, that he is directing the collection primarily at the young, eager musician (he may well have had a backward glance at his own childhood experiences), but he does not, quite rightly, exclude the older musicians, for they, too, were inexperienced in the newly-available keys. His words "for the use and profit" also tells us that he intended these pieces to be of practical help in developing performing skills and, besides, a useful addition to the repertoire in their own right. His judgement in these matters has been constantly vindicated over the past two and a half centuries.[14]

The significance of the Preludes and Fugues is by no means limited to their encompassing all the keys through the cycle of fifths, but lies equally in their artistic merit. The formal details never become repetitious, technicalities never dominate, and the means of expression are infinitely varied. The fugue is exhibited in manifold forms and the themes are equally distinctive in their individuality and their capacity for development. Thus,

111. The Well Tempered Clavier – title page, 1722, autograph.

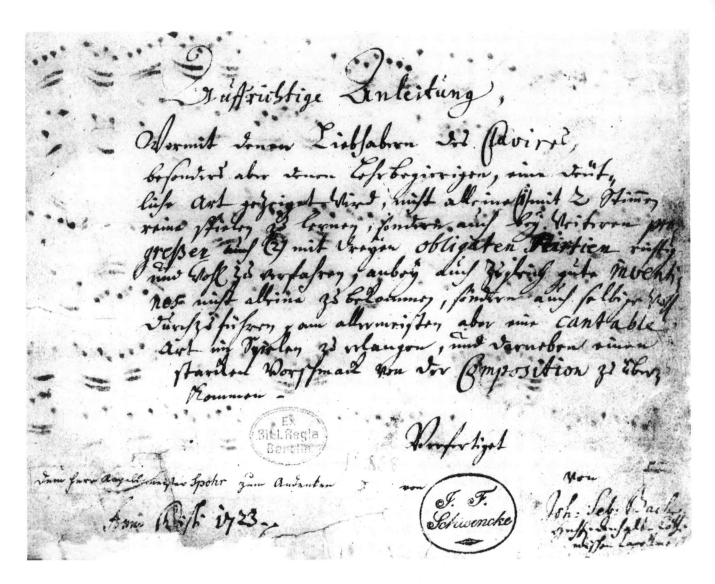

*112. Inventions –
title page, 1723,
autograph.*

the formal aspects of the fugue become a framework within which musical inventiveness of the most varied kinds appears.

Another of the great Bach collections is that of the two- and three-part Inventions. Dated 1723, the title page reads:

> Honest instruction, in which keyboard enthusiasts, but particularly those desirous of learning, will be shown clearly not only (1) to play clearly in two parts, but also, after they have made some progress, (2) to deal rightly and well with three obbligato parts; and furthermore not only to have good ideas but to develop them correctly, and above all to attain a cantabile style of playing and at the same time to acquire a strong taste for composition. Prepared by Joh: Seb: Bach, Kapellmeister at the court of His Highness the Prince of Anhalt-Cöthen.

The composer here puts forward a whole educational programme which shows us how Bach's conception progressed coherently from the studious interest to the performing skill to the ambition to compose, and saw the whole process as one desirable unity. We see him here, at the age of thirty-eight, requiring much the same from the keyboard player as his son Carl Philipp Emanuel was to demand in 1753 in his *Treatise on the true way of playing the Clavier*. The Inventions should not be performed as lifeless, mechanical pieces, but as dynamic, expressive music. Unfortunately too little attention has been paid to this over the years.

Bach certainly had a didactic aim in view when he prepared the *Clavier-Büchlein* for his son Wilhelm Friedemann in 1720 and also when he prepared the *Notebooks* for his second wife, Anna Magdalena, in 1722 and 1725 respectively. The four parts of the *Clavier-Übung* (1731–42) and the Chorale Preludes of his latter years in Leipzig, are also

not lacking in educational ambitions, nor is *The Art of Fugue*, at least when these works are considered as a medium for artistic skills specific to their respective genres. From all these works and collections we can see how close teaching was to Bach's heart, how deep-seated was the blend of artist and teacher, how profoundly he felt that instruction was the way to true artistic independence together with the union of composer and performer. Another invigorating characteristic of Bach as a teacher was his open-mindedness towards new developments that enabled him not merely to preserve tradition but to initiate successful new departures.

From the end of the eighteenth century to the present, Bach's works have proved an indispensable source of inspiration and instruction to his successors; he was, and is, the patriarchal figure, the musical educator of the entire western world.

113. The Well Tempered Clavier, Book One. Beginning of the Prelude in B flat minor, autograph.

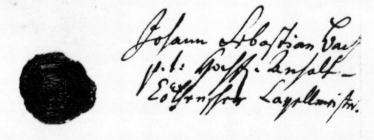

The Encyclopedist

The eighteenth century — the era of the Enlightenment — was characterized by an encyclopedic striving after knowledge in the arts and sciences. The bourgeois classes were beginning to emerge, and saw in the new dissemination of knowledge and the application of reason and understanding an "escape from man's self-inflicted immaturity" (*Kant*). The Enlightenment had its historical and philosophical roots in Renaissance humanism, in the Reformation, and in the writings of seventeenth-century rationalist philosophers such as Descartes, Spinoza, and Leibniz. In the field of music an increasing number of treatises and books about practice and theory appeared, making all the current knowledge of the art available. One may cite as examples Andreas Werckmeister's treatise on tuning according to mathematical principles (1686/7); the Frenchman Joseph Sauveur's *Principles of Acoustics* (1700/01); Jean Philippe Rameau's important *Treatise on Harmony* (1722); Johann David Heinichen's writings on thorough-bass (1711 and 1728), the various volumes of Johann Mattheson, notably *Der vollkommene Kapellmeister* (1739) and Johann Gottfried Walther's *Lexicon of Music* (1732), not to mention those that were written after 1740. Didacticism had become a methodological principle of the Enlightenment, and encyclopedic assemblages of knowledge such as these were very much in demand.

Bach left us no theoretical writings, no learned discourses; he even seems to have deliberately avoided committing his thoughts or his views on questions about music to paper. Yet his works, as well as much contemporary comment, show him to have been a cultivated, well-read man who never tired of seeking out information on those topics which were of importance to him. There was no field of composition in which he had not made himself thoroughly familiar with the works of other composers. He studied Buxtehude, Reinken, Böhm, Fischer, Stölzel, Heinichen, Pisendel and Zelenka, Couperin, Corelli, Vivaldi, and Albinoni — not to mention Handel and Telemann. This interest in other composers' works was fundamental to Bach's own work and completely in accord with his desire to make a comprehensive knowledge the basis of a comprehensive output. Thus, Bach's achievements are always linked to those of his predecessors and contemporaries.

There was no field of music which Bach considered irrelevant to his overall grasp of his art and his profession: whether as composer, performer, Kapellmeister, Cantor or teacher, his approach was universal and encyclopedic. He collected knowledge, endowed it with his own individuality, and communicated it. Early in his career he had begun to gather works of the same genre into collections — chorale preludes into the *Orgelbüchlein*, preludes and fugues into the *Well Tempered Clavier*, sets of keyboard suites,

115. Bach as Kapellmeister at Cöthen (?) – unauthenticated oil-painting by Johann Jakob Ihle.

sonatas and partitas for solo violin, concerti grossi, compilations of church cantatas, various kinds of keyboard works in the four parts of the *Clavier-Übung* (an encyclopedia of keyboard writing in its own right), fugues and canons into the *Musical Offering*, and, into *The Art of Fugue*, an examination of the potentialities within one form. The way in which he transcended the bounds of a particular genre so that an individual work could become a summary of the potentialities inherent in that genre, has already been discussed with particular reference to the *St Matthew Passion*, the *Mass in B minor*, and the *Christmas Oratorio*. In this sense, these works too were encyclopedic.

The development of Bach's career was conducive to comprehensive achievement in that it spanned so many areas of musical activity each with its specific demands. He was by turn chorister, organist, keyboard-player, continuo-player, court musician, Konzert-meister, Kapellmeister, and Cantor — and, throughout, composer. He was also an acknowledged expert in matters concerning the construction and the general techni-calities of the organ, the harpsichord, and the clavichord, he was a teacher and a publisher. He was, indeed, the epitome of the complete musician. It is hardly possible to assimilate so many different facets, or to reconstruct from such a varied mosaic the image of the man.

Was Bach himself conscious of all this? He was certainly a self-confident man who

116. Clavier-Übung,
Partita I, BWV 825
— title-page of the
first edition, 1726.

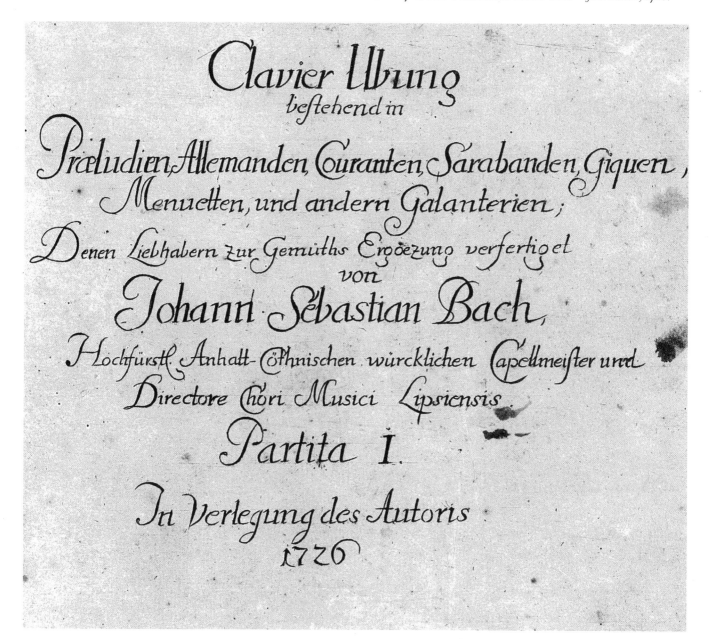

was well aware of his own ability and able to evaluate his knowledge and skill in relation to that of others. His constant striving for professional perfection and an all-round development of his capabilities is undeniable. In terms of professional employment, he always sought new challenges, new scope. Linked to this was his ever-increasing versatility in composition, which meant adapting himself to, and mastering new genres and exploring fresh forms whether vocal or instrumental, sacred or secular. The idea of watertight compartments in music was utterly foreign to him; he parodied freely between one genre and another, blending the sacred with the secular, fusing elements of the fugue, the sonata, the cantata, and the concerto. None of this was haphazard; rather was it the result of planning, of deliberate exploration of every conceivable potentiality of form and instrumentation to reveal new effects, a new essence within. In this way Bach was the most important exponent of the encyclopedic principle in the Enlightenment as far as music was concerned.

That the encyclopedic philosophy and religious faith were by no means mutually exclusive is shown nowhere as clearly as in the work of Bach, where we find Lutheran tenets, the spirit of Christianity, and enlightened bourgeois thought combined through the medium of music into a unity. It must be borne in mind that of all the arts, music was the most developed in eighteenth-century Germany, not least as the result of Bach's own contribution. The depths of characterization that one finds in his work, the ways of presenting intellectual ideas through music, the fusion of individuality and expressivity and the bold blend of tradition and innovation were all unprecedented.

And yet Bach was not an out-and-out "enlightener". There is no evidence of his ever having said anything to suggest that he was a social critic — unlike the later French encyclopedists — and he was no philosopher. Everything that he felt he expressed in his music. The man who wrote "Soli Deo Gloria" at the head of his compositions was a man of sincere and unshakeable faith, whose beliefs were not even endangered, let alone destroyed, by contemporary developments.

Remarkable indeed is the way in which Bach's life and works reflect the development of middle-class thought and feeling. Contemporary views on education, on the consolidation of work, on religion, all found a ready response with him, and the retention of the old while embracing the new, which was also a feature of the times, had its counterpart in his willingness to blend the traditional with the innovatory in his art. His own attitudes not only corresponded in the main to the particular historical conditions in which Bach grew up and in which he worked, but the great master was himself a "summary", the total of his works a "collection" of all that was most positive and most constructive in that period.

117. Aria in G major, the theme of the Goldberg Variations, BWV 988. Original edition.

118. Leipzig – Bach memorial by Carl Seffner, 1908.

The Heritage

Our attitude towards history is constantly changing. As the times, the events, and the achievements are evaluated according to different, subjective criteria, so our perspective alters. Even so, as knowledge about the events of the past, about the conditions in which the people of a given epoch lived, viewed their world and changed it becomes more complete, gradually a basis for a better understanding is built up. This has certainly been the case with the life and work of Johann Sebastian Bach.

Since the middle of the nineteenth century, when scholars became seriously interested in him, more and more of Bach's works have been discovered and studied and documents pertaining to his life have been collected and investigated. Many works and documents have been irretrievably lost and there may be many others still to be found, but even so the knowledge about him has been steadily increasing over the years and the volume of his works which is now available is enormous.

The further we move away from the time in which he lived, the more difficult it becomes to understand and evaluate the conditions of his times, his life and work and the personal characteristics of the man. It is a strange fact, but it seems that the more we learn about Bach the more questions we find to ask. Given the complexity of the subject and the lively state of the research, this is, perhaps, only to be expected.

The view that Bach's music was consigned to oblivion immediately after the composer's death and only rediscovered thanks to a memorable performance of the *St Matthew Passion* by the young Felix Mendelssohn in 1829 was discredited many decades ago. To a certain extent Bach's music was swept aside by the onrush of new developments during the course of the eighteenth century as younger composers, from Bach's own sons to the classical Viennese masters, came to the fore with their quite different ideas about music, but his reputation and a few of his works were well known throughout the European musical world.

His sons and his pupils possessed either the originals or copies of many of his compositions and helped to disperse them, though not in any great numbers, by making further copies. Many of Bach's works existed in no other form than in such copies. In Vienna, Baron von Swieten possessed some of Bach's compositions and both Mozart and Beethoven came to know them there. Haydn's estate included some works by Bach. Beethoven studied *The Well Tempered Clavier* when taking lessons with Neefe in Bonn, and we know that when Mozart visited Leipzig, Doles, the Cantor at St Thomas's, showed him some motets by Bach. From 1764 onwards the Leipzig publishing house of Breitkopf listed numerous works by Bach in the catalogue. At the end of the eighteenth century, interest in Bach's works had grown sufficiently for a stop to be put to the casual dissipation

119. Leipzig – Bach memorial, 1843, donated by Mendelssohn.

of the Bach heritage through the selling off of individual pieces and they began to be collected and compiled. An important part in this was played by, among others, Johann Nikolaus Forkel, Friedrich Zelter, Georg Poelchau, and Siegfried Dehn. As German national consciousness became established in the early nineteenth century, interest in history and in the achievements of the past became more evident and gave rise to greater attention being paid to artists and their works. One of the results of this movement was the first biography of Bach, published in 1802. The author, Forkel, had direct access to Bach's heirs and Carl Philipp Emanuel was particularly helpful. Forkel, who was influenced by the eighteenth-century Enlightenment, declared Bach's memory to be a matter of national importance. Interest in Bach can be traced through Carl Friedrich Fasch, the founder of the Berlin Singakademie, through Friedrich Zelter to Zelter's pupil Mendelssohn, who, under the aegis of his teacher, gave the first performance of the *St Matthew Passion* since Bach's death — on the centenary of the work's first performance in 1729. Bach's works have always held their place in the repertoire of the choir of St Thomas's in Leipzig. Johann Friedrich Doles, the Cantor there from 1756–89, was a Bach pupil, and later Cantors such as Johann Adam Hiller, August Eberhard Müller, and Johann Gottfried Schicht all proved to be worthy trustees of the Bach legacy.

In 1849 the Bach Society was founded in England and in 1850 the Bachgesellschaft was formed in Leipzig, its aim being to compile a complete edition of the composer's works. That this great enterprise should have been undertaken is a clear proof of how interest in Bach had grown — on all sides — in the one hundred years after his death. Actively associated with the Bachgesellschaft were such names as Thomascantor Moritz Hauptmann, Otto Jahn, Siegfried Dehn, Ignaz Moscheles, Carl von Winterfeld, Robert Schumann, Franz Liszt, and Philipp Spitta. Fifty years went by before the editors were able to bring the great work to completion. The biography of Bach by Philipp Spitta has long served as a basic contribution to our knowledge both through the comprehensive portraits he gives of the man and the inclusion of many letters and documents which provide an historical background. The process of research continues today and we are discovering more and more about Bach and his work. The process gives rise, however, to distinct shifts in emphasis. Previously, in keeping with the romanticized view of history, the strongest emphasis was upon Bach as a church musician and scant attention was paid to the instrumental works and the secular vocal compositions — exceptions being made for such collections as *The Well Tempered Clavier* and the organ pieces. Only later was due attention paid to the whole astonishing gamut of his works.

As his works became better known in the nineteenth century, so did his influence upon other composers gain momentum until he came to be regarded as the doyen of

120. Collected edition of Bach's works – volume I, Leipzig 1851, title page.

composers, the musician from whom anyone who took music seriously had to learn. Mendelssohn, Schumann, Liszt, Brahms, Wagner, Reger, Schoenberg, Stravinsky, Hindemith, Eisler, and Shostakovich all acknowledged a debt to "old" Bach. Together with many others they learned from his supreme craftsmanship, revered the inexhaustible riches of his works and were stimulated or inspired by his genius. Some, as a gesture of homage, even composed works based upon the theme suggested by the letters of his name. Bach's music now achieved an unequalled universality.

On 27 January 1900, the concluding volume of the complete works of the great Thomascantor was laid before the Committee of the Bachgesellschaft in Leipzig and the Society was dissolved, its aim fulfilled. But now that all his works (as far as they knew at the time) had been found, a new task arose: that of reviving them and having them regularly performed. Thus, on the very same day, 27 January 1900, a New Bachgesellschaft (NBG) was founded in Leipzig. Its goal was that of making Bach's music known to as wide a public as possible, the immediate emphasis being placed upon the sacred works. The methods were various and imaginative. The NBG established an annual Bach festival, and in 1907 opened the *Bachhaus*, a museum dedicated to Bach, in the house on the Frauenplan in Eisenach that was reputed to be his birthplace. In 1905 they instituted the *Bachjahrbuch*, an annual publication of research into Bach. These were fine ventures, all sparked off by great enthusiasm and a sincere sense of responsibility. The Society's aims thus covered not only the performance, but the analysis and interpretation of Bach's music, its publication in good performing editions and the uncovering of new sources of knowledge about it. These aims were reflected by Albert Schweitzer in his widely-read book *J. S. Bach* which appeared in French in 1905 and in German in 1908. As a comprehensive portrayal of the composer, it helped to reveal the man and his music to countless readers. Another seminal work was André Pirro's *L'esthétique de J. S. Bach* (1907), though today both distinguished works are somewhat antiquated because of their excessive hermeneutics.

Leipzig was now firmly established as the centre of the movement to initiate performances of Bach's music and stimulate Bach research on the broadest possible basis. It

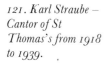

121. Karl Straube – Cantor of St Thomas's from 1918 to 1939.

122. Right. Günther Ramin – Cantor of St Thomas's from 1940 to 1956.

was in Leipzig that the Cantor Karl Straube, a man with a deep sense of commitment and responsibility towards Bach, began, in 1918, to give consistent performances of the cantatas, oratorios, motets and organ pieces; the performances of the choir of St Thomas's under his direction excited enormous interest in many countries. Leipzig, too, was the home of the publishers who first printed and distributed Bach's work and who continued to consider it an essential part of their responsibilities. The town was also the venue for a great number of Bach festivals which allowed singers and instrumentalists with a special interest in Bach to display their artistry and skill. Bach's music was now not simply available, but was being performed throughout the musical world. It was an accepted and vital element of culture in the widest sense.

The year 1950 was particularly important for the Bach cult. It was the bicentenary of the master's death, and with the horror of the Nazi years and the destructions of the Second World War now over, it was celebrated by a great festival during which Leipzig,

123. Leipzig, St Thomas's Church – the choir singing under the direction of their Cantor, Hans-Joachim Rotzsch.

Bach's home town, staged new performaces, a conference of musicologists and an international competition for young Bach players.

At the same time, the *Neue Bach-Ausgabe* (The New Bach Edition) was initiated. A collaboration between the Bach scholars of many different countries, its editorial direction comes from the Bach Archive in Leipzig, which was also founded in 1950, and from the Bach Institute in Göttingen. Werner Neumann, Alfred Dürr, and Georg von Dadelsen have been particularly closely associated with the venture. There are hopes that this work may be completed by the end of the century. If this is so, it will have taken fifty years — exactly the same time that it took for the first edition of Bach's works to appear. The Bach bicentenary celebrations of 1950 had many important repercussions. The prejudices which favoured some aspects of his work at the expense of others were gradually eliminated and his achievement as a whole was more appreciated. New research into the circumstances of his life and the genesis of his works was undertaken and provided further insight into performance techniques — an immensely valuable stimulus for the performers themselves. The upsurge of interest in authentic instruments of the time — harpsichord, viola da gamba, oboe d'amore, among others — and their associated playing techniques, has allowed performers to get away from the nineteenth-century sound and to discover one that approximates to that of Bach's own time. The size and disposition of the forces used has also been adjusted with great effect. The availability of documents in Bach's own writing and the commentaries written during the first half-century after his death have proved of invaluable assistance to the endeavours of the musicologists. They have been published in book form both in German and English.

In order to keep abreast of world-wide developments, the Neue Bachgesellschaft became an international organization in 1970, with Leipzig retained as its traditional base. It has long been an accepted practice for chamber music ensembles, orchestras and choirs to incorporate the name of Bach into their titles, and the number of societies, schools, institutes and music competitions that have adopted his name is countless — and an acknowledgement, in every instance, of indebtedness to the great master.

Bach has become an integral part of our education, his works forming not only the core of our musical heritage but an individual link with the past. For some, Bach represents a venerated ideal, the epitome of musical genius; for others he represents the taskmaster imposing bitter toil before conferring the longed-for joy of assimilation. In spite of all that has been done, there are still many people to whom Bach's music remains inaccessible. Sooner or later many more will experience its astonishing power. For some, the hour of their meeting with Bach will come only after a prolonged period of peace and friendly co-operation has provided the right climate for the growth of culture, the arts and knowledge throughout the world.

遂に実現した待望の豪華公演！

J.S.バッハ

マタイ受難曲

全曲演奏会

J.S.Bach＝MATTHÄUSPASSION

待望の
横浜公演!!

現在望みうる最高の演奏陣！

ライプツィヒ聖トーマス教会合唱団
ドレスデン・フィルハーモニー管弦楽団

ソプラノ●レギーナ・ヴェルナー　アルト●ギゼラ・ポール　テノール（福音史家）●ディーター・ヴァイマン
バス（キリスト）●ヘルマン＝クリスティアーン・ボルスター　バス●ゴットハルト・シュティアー

指揮●第30代教会合唱長ハンス＝ヨアヒム・ローチュ

Thomanerchor Leipzig
Dresdner Philharmonie

Sopran●Regina Werner　Alt●Gisela Pohl　Tenor(Evangelist)●Dieter Weimann
Bass(Christus)●Hermann-Christian Polster　Bass●Gothart Stier
Dirigent●Hans＝Joachim Rotzsch

6月24日(火)6時開演　神奈川県立音楽堂

Tue., Jun. 24 at 6:00P.M.　KANAGAWA KENRITU ONGAKUDOU

入場料 S＝¥5,000　A＝¥4,000　B＝¥3,300　C＝¥2,800　D＝¥2,300
主催＝神奈川県立音楽堂・総合文化社　後援＝ドイツ民主共和国大使館

市内各プレイガイドにて絶賛前売中!! お問合せ・御予約は(045)231-8635神奈川県立音楽堂・(03)405-1171総合文化社

124. First Japanese Bach Festival, 1975, with the participation of the choir of St Thomas's.

125. Bach's tomb at St Thomas's – his sarcophagus has been there since 1949.

Notes

1 Page 15. It was customary in Germany to publish a eulogy (*Nekrolog*) upon the death of a distinguished person. An elaborate eulogy was indeed written and it is a valuable document for historians.

2 Page 23. There is no point quoting the exact sums paid to Bach; we do not know the purchasing power of thalers and florins, and thus the figures are meaningless to us.

3 Page 27. See this, as well as all other large quotations in excellent English translations in *The Bach Reader*, New York 1945.

4 Page 34. It should be noted, however, that the transcriptions were made for unaccompanied harpsichord, a virtually new genre.

5 Page 36. Though this encounter is fairly well documented, these artistic tournaments seem to have occurred from antiquity to the nineteenth century, and all of them sound similar.

6 Page 44. Over the years Anna Magdalena's handwriting came to resemble her husband's.

7 Full text in *The Bach Reader*.

8 Page 69. The reason for this was a very successful staged performance on the occasion of the hundredth anniversary of the Freiburg Gymnasium. The music was provided by J. F. Doles, a pupil of Bach's.

9 Page 119. The establishment of the vitally important chronology we owe to Walter Dürr in 1976, but it will take some time before the correct numbering of the cantatas will be generally accepted.

10 Page 133. The best summary explanation of the St John Passion can be found in the critical appendix to Arthur Mendel's edition of the Passion in the New Bach Edition.

11 Page 141. Widely known from the famous *Florilegium Portense*, a collection of motets published by Eberhard Bodenschatz in two parts, 1602 and 1621.

12 Page 143. In the estate of Emanuel Bach, who inherited the score of the Mass, the work is called "the great Catholic Mass".

13 Page 153. Modern critical edition with ample commentary by Christoph Wolff in 1977.

14 Page 160. However, contrary to popular belief it was neither Werckmeister nor *The Well Tempered Clavier* that established equal temperament. It has been in use since the Renaissance and Bach even had predecessors who composed such anthologies, if nothing comparable to his achievement.

Picture sources and acknowledgements

BA Bacharchiv Leipzig (Bach archive), the national centre in the German Democratic Republic for the commemoration of Bach and research into his life and work.

DFD Deutsche Fotothek Dresden (German photographic library).

DSB Deutsche Staatsbibliothek Berlin (German State Library, Berlin).

MBL Musikbibliothek der Stadt Leipzig (Leipzig municipal music library).

MGL Museum für Geschichte der Stadt Leipzig (Leipzig municipal museum of history).

NaFoGe Nationale Forschungs- und Gedenkstätten der Klassischen Deutschen Literatur Weimar (National centre for the commemoration of and research into classical German literature).

SAL Stadtarchiv Leipzig (Leipzig town archives).

SLB Sächsische Landesbibliothek (Saxon regional library).

SPK Staatsbibliothek Preussischer Kulturbesitz, West Berlin (State library of the Prussian cultural heritage).

UB Universitätsbibliothek (University library).

ZDKW Zentralbibliothek der Deutschen Klassik Weimar (Central library of German classicism, Weimar).

Frontispiece: Oil painting by Elias Gottlob Haussmann, Leipzig 1746, MGL.

1. Published by Homann's heirs, 1734, BA
2. BA
3. Photo, 1983, Werner Reinhold
4. Topographia, 1650
5. Photo, 1983, Werner Reinhold
6. Photo, 1983, Werner Reinhold
7. Engraving by Jakon von Sandrat, 1690, after Wilhelm Richter
8. NaFoGe
9. Photo, Rolf Langematz
10. Oil painting, probably by Johann David Herlicius, DSB
11. Eisenach, St George's church register
12. Ohrdruf local museum
13. Engraving in Merian's Topographia, 1654
14. Lithograph c.1840, Bomann Museum, Celle
15. Merian, Topographia, 1654
16. Photo, 1982, Werner Reinhold
17. Engraving by Pius Rösel of Rosenhoff, c.1700, after Meister Wolf, c.1570; Arnstadt, palace museum
18. Lithograph, 1847, L. Spilhans, plan of Lübeck
19. Photo, 1983, Werner Reinhold
20. Photo, 1982, Werner Reinhold
21. Arnstadt town archives
22. Engraving in Merian's Topographia, 1650
23. Dornheim church register from the Arnstadt church archive
24. Photo, 1982, Werner Reinhold
25. BA, on permanent loan from MBL
26. DSB
27. Photo, 1983, Werner Reinhold
28. Etching after Georg Melchior Kraus, DSB
29. SKW, Photo by Louis Held
30. BA
31. Erfurt town museum, photo by Rolf Langematz
32. Engraving by Johann Westhofer after Friedrich Daniel Bretschneider
33. Engraving by Gabriel Bodenehr the Elder, 1715, DSB
34. DSB
35. DSB
36. DFD
37. Etching by Canaletto, 1750, DFD
38. Weimar State archives
39. Engraving in Merian's Topographia, 1650

40. Oil painting, Cöthen local museum, photo by Rolf Langematz
41. Anonymous engraving, DSB
42. DSB
43. DSB
44. SPK
45. Photo, 1983, Werner Reinhold
46. Engraving by Johann Georg Schreiber, 1712, BA, photo by Rolf Langematz
47. MGL
48. Engraving by Martin Bernigeroth, BA
49. Photo, 1983, Werner Reinhold
50. Oil painting by Alexander Thiele, 1740, MGL, photo by Gerhard Reinhold
51. Wood engraving by O. Kutschera after Hubert Kratz
52. Coloured engraving by Johann Georg Schreiber, BA
53. DSB
54. BA, on permanent loan from the former Leipzig town library
55. Engraving by Johann Christoph Oberdörffer, BA, photo by Rolf Langematz
56. Oil painting by Elias Gottlob Haussmann, c.1725, MGL
57. SPK
58. Engraving by Lorenzo Zucchi, MGL
59. Engraving by Lorenzo Zucchi, DSB
60. DFD
61. MBL
62. MBL
63. Engraving, MGL
64. Engraving, DSB
65. Engraving, DSB
66. Coloured drawing, DSB
67. DSB
68. Pastel drawing by Gottlieb Friedrich Bach, Bach House, Eisenach, photo by Rolf Langematz
69. Pastel drawing by Gottlieb Friedrich Bach, Bach House, Eisenach, photo by Rolf Langematz
70. BA
71. DSB
72. DSB
73. Photo, 1983, Werner Reinhold
74. Photo, 1983, Werner Reinhold
75. BA, photo by Rolf Langematz
76. Musical instrument museum of the Karl Marx University, Leipzig, photo, 1983, Werner Reinhold
77. Palace museum of local history, Sondershausen, photo, 1983, Werner Reinhold
78. DSB
79. Engraving after Johann Georg Schreiber, MGL
80. Water-colour, Hamburg museum of art and trade
81. DSB
82. Copper engraving by Rudolph Holzhalb, Zürich central library
83. Engraving, Leipzig, 1727
84. DSB
85. Photo, 1983, Werner Reinhold
86. Engraving by Johann Gottfried Krügner the Elder, 1717
87. UB Leipzig
88. Gouache by Christian Richter, c.1660, SKW, photo by Louis Held
89. Weimar, 1715, DSB
90. Weimar/Jena, 1717, ZDKW
91. Engraving by Johann Gottfried Krügner the Elder, 1723, BA
92. First Edition, Leipzig, 1732
93. First Edition, Leipzig, 1732
94. DSB
95. Lithograph, c.1850
96. DSB
97. Photo, 1983, Werner Reinhold
98. SPK
99. DSB
100. BA
101. BA
102. SLB
103. Engraving by Johann Georg Schreiber, MGL
104. SLB, destroyed in the War
105. DSB
106. Violin from the collection of St Thomas's Church, Leipzig; Flute from the musical instrument museum of the Karl Marx University, Leipzig, photo, 1983, Werner Reinhold
107. DSB
108. State palaces and gardens – Potsdam, photo, 1983, Werner Reinhold
109. Private collection
110. Photo, 1983, Werner Reinhold
111. DSB
112. DSB
113. DSB
114. SAL
115. Oil painting, c.1720(?), Bach House, Eisenach, photo by Rolf Langematz
116. DSB
117. Photo, 1983, Werner Reinhold
118. Photo, 1983, Werner Reinhold
119. Steel engraving by Albert Henry Payne, c.1850
120. Photo, 1983
121. Oil painting by Amalie Baumann, photo by Rolf Langematz
122. MGL, photo by K. Plathen
123. Photo, 1983, Werner Reinhold
124. BA
125. Photo, 1983, Werner Reinhold

Index